MISSION POSSIBLE

MISSION POSSIBLE

The Story of the Latin American
Agribusiness Development Corporation
(LAAD)

Robert L. Ross

Transaction Publishers
New Brunswick (U.S.A.) and London (U.K.)

Copyright © 2000 by Transaction Publishers, New Brunswick, New Jersey.

This book is printed on acid-free paper that meets the American National Standard for Permanence of Paper for Printed Library Materials.

Library of Congress Catalog Number: 99-057800
ISBN: 0-7658-0035-7 (cloth)
Printed in the United States of America

Library of Congress Cataloging-in-Publication Data

Ross, Robert L.
    Mission possible : the story of the Latin America Agribusiness Corporation (LAAD) / by Robert L. Ross.
        p. cm.
    Includes index.
    ISBN 0-7658-0035-7 (alk. paper)
        1. Latin American Agribusiness Development Corporation—History.   2. Agricultural development projects—Latin America.   3. Agricultural assistance, American—Latin America.   4. Enterprise Zones, Rural—Latin America.
        I. Title.
HD1790.5 .R67 2000
331.1'88—dc21   99-057800

To
Tom Mooney

Without whom, we
would not have made it

Contents

Foreword   ix

Preface   xi

Introduction   1

1. Poverty and the Cold War   9

2. An Idea is Born   15

3. The Players   23

4. The Game Begins   41

5. From Childhood to Adolescence   53

6. The Real World   65

7. A New Lease on Life   83

8. The Bottom Line: Development   101

9. The Bottom Line: Profitability and Risk   119

10. Development, Politics, and the Human Factor   135

Appendix A: LAAD's Directors by Shareholder   145

Appendix B: Geographic Distribution of Projects   149

Appendix C: Economic Distribution of Projects   150

Appendix D: Financial Indicators, 1970-98   151

Index   153

Foreword

All successful companies have a story to tell. The Latin American Agribusiness Development Corporation has its own and it is a very special one. For this reason, the Board of Directors wanted to put it in writing so that future generations of employees, directors and clients would know about the pioneer years of this great little enterprise.

LAAD has a very rich tradition, obtained through almost thirty years of dedication, innovation, flexibility in dealing with difficult situations, and mainly perseverance, without which we would not have survived these difficult first years. Robert Ross, LAAD's president since 1972, provided excellent leadership during most of the life of the company. As he approached retirement, the Board decided this was a golden opportunity to have the company history written by the person most qualified to do so.

For those interested in modern Latin American history and evolution, reading this book is a must. These are the historic facts as seen through the eyes of a small financial company at the mercy of the always volatile Latin American marketplace. The destiny of LAAD was so dependent on the Latin American economies that their histories largely dictated our own and this influence will continue as long as the company exists.

We thought our story worth telling. We sincerely hope you will enjoy reading it.

Gonzalo J. Dal Borgo
Chairman of the Board

Preface

I wrote this book at the request of my Board of Directors. It narrates the nearly thirty-year history of an unusual company created for the purpose of financing and encouraging private agribusiness enterprises in Latin America. The Latin American Agribusiness Development Corporation, better known as LAAD, was a creation of corporate America. Latin America is, after all, a major market for American agribusiness.

At its inception, LAAD represented a challenging idea with a modest capital base. Even today, it remains small by American standards. Thirty years later, its cumulative impact on the region is statistically barely measurable. Yet, in agriculture, the story was quite different. By focusing its efforts, LAAD was able to play a significant role in financing the small players in what has become an agricultural revolution in Latin America. Our clients were the frontline fighters in this revolution. People were our real business. LAAD may be judged by numbers, but it is individual work that creates them.

I begin this book by describing the world as it was when our shareholders decided to form this venture thirty years ago. They lived in a very different world from now, one full of conflict and ideological rivalry. The world was divided into three major ideological camps, each jockeying for position and advantage. Many American business leaders sought ways of engaging themselves and their companies constructively in this conflict.

This book focuses on the key actors, including clients, directors, and management. This is above all their story. The book contains an approximate chronology of events, but I have tried to use the chronology to illustrate a point or to highlight the individual clients we financed.

I undertook to measure and analyze the results both in terms of development and of the financial performance of the company. The reader will find no theoretical advance in his understanding of the development process. He will find how one company coped with an idealistic mission in a real world of financial crises, political uncertainty, civil unrest, and volatile commodity markets.

This book also has much to do with my professional career, involving over twenty-six of the thirty-eight years I spent in the field of Latin America's economic development. Trained in the ideologies and languages of the Cold War, to me the challenges of developing the Third World easily outweighed the directionless nuclear stalemate of the two superpowers.

In 1960, David Pollock, a Canadian economist in charge of the U.N. Economic Commission for Latin America's (ECLA) Washington office, hired me as his assistant. David taught me my first lessons on Latin American theories of economic development. This assignment coincided with the launching of the Alliance for Progress, the first American policy of constructive engagement in Latin America following the end of World War II. President John F. Kennedy was faced with his first Cold War challenge in the Western Hemisphere following Fidel Castro's taking power in Cuba. Seeking the moral high ground, he consulted Latin American leaders and economists, who recommended that the United States take a strong stand in favor of economic and social reform. The most influential of the Latin America leaders was Dr. Raul Prebisch, the head of ECLA. He argued persuasively that the region was falling behind economically because of "structural rigidities" in a region dependent on supplying raw materials to the world and receiving high value goods in exchange. Dr. Prebisch's ideas provided the ideological underpinning to the Alliance for Progress.

The Alliance chose to send a major planning mission to the region's poorest country - Haiti and I was hired as the assistant to the mission chief. Designing a plan proved a relatively easy task in a primitive environment, but implementing it proved impossible. The Haitian government was rife with incompetence and corruption.

In 1962, Dr. Prebisch sent me to Chile to teach at the U.N.'s Institute for Economic and Social Planning. Upon arrival, I was given three weeks to prepare myself in Spanish, a language I barely understood. I spent three years teaching and doing research on economic development, including half a year working with Paraguay's Central Bank helping to prepare that country's first development plan. Economic planning and social reform were at the top of everyone's priority list in Latin America in those days. People believed that government planning could help jumpstart the region's stagnating economies. The rhetoric rang strong, but at my humble level, I was hard pressed to find any concrete accomplishment from my very hard work.

In the spring of 1965, I was offered a job in Peru with the Adela Investment Company. Adela had been formed the previous year by a group of multinational corporations from around the world to promote venture capital in Latin America. The company hired me as its staff economist, a job that took me around much of Latin America evaluating investment opportunities. Here was a company that risked its own capital along with local investors in building new production facilities. The company quickly expanded its operations to the entire region growing eventually to nearly half of a billion dollars, a considerable sum in those days.

This became my new world. Venture capital and project financing were at the forefront of developing Latin America in a more direct way than was ever possible in government planning offices. Adela had its successes and failures, but it was always in the front line and its executives all learned valuable lessons from that experience.

In the spring of 1972, I was offered the presidency of LAAD by its chairman, Paul Cornelsen, who was also the executive vice president of Ralston Purina International.

Some months before receiving this offer, Ralston Purina's Chilean subsidiary was intervened by the Chilean government under President Salvador Allende. Ralston Purina and the Chilean government hired Adela as a mediator. I was asked to negotiate with the American side, while Adela's Santiago representative, Edmundo Miquel, negotiated with the Chileans. An agreement was soon reached and signed by all the parties, thereby ending one of the first flash points in the growing tension between the leftist Chilean government and the American administration.

Just prior to the signing, the LAAD Board of Directors had asked Mr. Cornelsen to hire a new president for LAAD. The timing proved to be for-tuitous, as he gave me the first option to take the job. Before accepting, I flew to Mexico City to meet LAAD's representative there, Bruce Berckmans and then on to Guatemala City to talk to Thomas Mooney, a friend and former colleague from Adela days. I frankly harbored doubts about LAAD's viability be-cause of its small capital base and I hoped to dispel my doubts. It was Tom, who with his typical ebul-lience, persuaded me that the company could suc-ceed based on a $6 million long term loan he had negotiated for LAAD with the U.S. Agency for International Development. I accepted the offer.

I submitted several drafts of this book to people who knew us best. Benjamin Fernandez, my suc-cessor, and a LAAD executive for over twenty years mercifully saved the reader having to wade through an ideological analysis that is anachronis-tic in today's world. Oscar Alvarez, our treasurer, with the company for twenty years, brought his prodigious memory to shore up my failing one. J. Hunter Martin, our regional vice president and an English major from the University of Virginia, finally took his revenge after years of my correct-ing his loan proposals. Carlos Julio Ravelo, also a regional vice president, reminded me repeatedly to give maximum attention to the people we did business with.

Among our directors, Ricardo Robles from Cargill went through the draft with his customary thoroughness. Fred Sutton from Monsanto and Warren Leonard from Chase both helped set the record straight many years after the events.

Most importantly, Tom Mooney wrote his own draft of this book based on his long personal knowledge of individual clients and projects. Many of the examples cited in this book were drawn from his draft.

In the end, of course, I take full responsibility for any and all shortcomings. I hope they are few and outweighed by the historical record and insights of one company's perspective of Latin America's postwar development.

Introduction

The Cold War may seem like an unlikely beginning to our story, but it is. In 1962, then Senator Jacob Javits, Republican of New York, speaking at a NATO parliamentary meeting in Paris, called on private business in the industrialized world to take the initiative in assisting private enterprise in what was then called the Third World. He argued that the development institutions of the free world were government controlled and that multinational corporations were better suited to promote private entrepreneurship in the poorer nations of the non-Communist world.

At the time of his speech, virtually all of the financial assistance being channeled to the Third World was provided by international development institutions like the World Bank, the United Nations specialized agencies and bilateral aid agencies of individual governments, such as the U.S. Agency for International Development. Western companies were investing for their own account in the Third World, but Senator Javits was calling on them to cooperate in stimulating local private enterprise as a matter of enlightened self-interest. The Second World (the Communists and their allies) sought to expropriate and collectivize private property in the Third World as a way of weakening its rivals in the First World (the industrialized democracies). Its reasoning was ideological and

1

political/military. Private enterprise worldwide was very much at the center of the Cold War debate.

Senator Javits' speech attracted the attention of key world business leaders, including George Moore of the United States, Marcus Wallenberg of Sweden, Gianno Agnelli of Italy and Frederik Philips of the Netherlands and many more. They, in turn, encouraged other corporate leaders from around the industrialized world to join. Over time, four separate private companies were formed and funded by large multinational corporations for the sole purpose of financing and encouraging private enterprise in the Third World.

The first of these, the Adela Investment Company (Adela) was incorporated in Luxembourg in 1964. Its focus was venture capital in Latin America. Within months, the new company had hired a managing director, Ernst Keller of Switzerland, and had established its head offices in Lima, Peru.

Within a few years, three more companies were incorporated and capitalized around the world. The Private Investment Company for Asia (PICA) set up its headquarters in Tokyo. The Societe Internationale pour le Financement de l'Investisement en Afrique (SIFIDA) operated out of Geneva, Switzerland. Finally, the subject of this book, the Latin American Agribusiness Development Corporation (LAAD) held its first Board of Directors meeting in New York City in January, 1970.

The largest of these companies was Adela, which pioneered the concept. It was initially capitalized at $16 million, but quickly doubled that figure. It eventually included 220 of the world's largest corporations from North and South America, Western

Europe and Japan. Ownership was carefully regu-
lated to prevent any one company from controlling
Adela. It was truly a multinational initiative and it
attracted professionals and executives from around
the world. It operated throughout Latin America
and the Caribbean. It specialized in providing venture capital to new and expanding businesses in a
wide range of economic activities, but it also provided technical, managerial and underwriting services
to the region. It sought to invest as a minority shareholder in new businesses and then sell its shares locally
once the business became profitable. It set up offices
throughout the region. Adela's assets quickly grew in
response to the shortage of venture capital in Latin
America. They eventually peaked at almost $500
million in the mid-nineteen seventies.

The smallest was LAAD. It was capitalized at
$2.4 million and was also designed to operate in
the same countries as Adela. Its primary mission
was to strengthen private agribusiness enterprises
in Latin America. Its shareholders were twelve
multinational agribusiness and financial institutions
with major trading and investment interests in Latin
America. Its intended market was the entire
agribusiness sector from farm production to retail
marketing. Its intended clients were medium and
small agribusiness firms.

The founding shareholders were:

> The Adela Investment Company *
> Bank of America N.T. & S.A.
> Borden Inc.
> Cargill, Inc.
> Caterpillar Tractor Company *
> CPC International Inc.

Dow Chemical Company *
Gerber Products Company
Deere & Company
Monsanto Company
Ralston Purina Company
Standard Fruit and Steamship Company
*Indicates shareholders who later sold their shares back to LAAD.

Subsequently, five more corporations joined, including Chase Manhattan Bank of New York City, Girard Bank of Philadelphia, Goodyear Tire and Rubber Company of Akron, Ohio, Rabobank Nederland of Utrecht, the Netherlands, and Southeast Banking Corporation of Miami, Florida. Girard Bank was subsequently bought by Mellon Bank, which sold its shares back to LAAD. The company repurchased all of the shares held by Southeast Banking Corporation from a bankruptcy court following a public auction.

Over the years since its inception, LAAD evolved from a wish list of good intentions to a profitable corporation specialized in financing agribusiness investment projects in a competitive world. LAAD has faced all of the business risks associated with agriculture, such as weather, market fluctuations, and physical isolation; the personal risks of working in countries racked by insurrection, kidnapping, and murder; the political risks associated with expropriation and exchange control; the economic risks of inflation and devaluation; the legal risks of operating in over twenty judicial systems; and the managerial risk of operating in twenty-five countries, each with its own business ethics and practices. Dealing with these risks in the real world has been the daily fare of management and directors.

LAAD's mission of promoting private investment in rural areas has remained unchanged from its first board of directors meeting until this day. Although LAAD operates as a private, for-profit company, the developmental mission of the company remains paramount when selecting projects and clients. Managers and directors debate development strategies and periodically review the economic and social impact of our investment activities. We had to stay focused both on our primary mission as well as our need for financial viability. LAAD had to be profitable in order to pay back its obligations and to grow. Profits were also necessary to motivate management to improve its performance. But, above all, profits were important to show that agriculture in Latin America is viable and bankable despite its reputation of high risk.

During this period, Latin America itself evolved from an inward-looking region to becoming an active participant in global trade. State tutelage gave way to private initiative. Agriculture recovered from decades of stagnation and agrarian reform to become a dynamic partner in the region's economic growth. The rebirth of Latin America's agriculture took years to accomplish and had to overcome periodic financial and political crises. It was measurably helped by the long trade negotiations, which eventually led to the creation of the World Trade Organization.

As LAAD nears its thirtieth anniversary, those three busy decades are still fresh in our memory. We still remember the early debates about priorities, the agonizingly slow start-up, the painstaking search for financial resources, the civil unrest in Central America, the Mexican default and instability in the commodities markets. But in the end, LAAD managed to leverage the original $2.4 million shareholders' equity and disburse $300 million in funding to some 700 private agribusiness projects in twenty-four Latin American and Caribbean nations. Thus, the shareholders' seed capital was leveraged 125 times over twenty-nine years, and the company's growth in loans and earnings continues to accelerate.

LAAD-financed projects are estimated to be generating over $500 million in yearly new hard currency earnings and to have created over 50,000 new jobs, most of them in rural areas. This has been the bottom line from the shareholders' perspective.

Financially, the company's annual earnings, after loan loss provisions, exceed $4 million, almost double the shareholders' initial equity investment Dividends have been paid to the shareholders for twenty years. The dividend rate now exceeds 40 percent of the par value of the shares.

Historically, the Bank of America is credited with being both the intellectual author of the LAAD concept as well as the syndicator of the original shareholder group. Few people may remember, but the Bank of America was very much an agribusiness bank in its formative growth years. Within the bank, Fred Orth, vice president in charge of agribusiness, first proposed it to his bank and he received early support from Bill Bolin, the vice president in charge of Latin America.

Fred argued that agriculture presented unique problems which merited specialized attention. He defined his market sector as being agribusiness, in recognition of the close link between production agriculture and agroindustry in the modern world. He followed the shareholder structure of Adela, PICA, and SIFIDA with a broad based support from the corporate world, companies with specialized knowledge in agribusiness as well as extensive investment and trading ties with Latin America.

The bank began to sound out some of its corporate clients in the agribusiness field and the proposal was positively received. The bank was quickly joined by CPC International, Inc. (now Best Foods), Deere & Company and Ralston Purina Company. Those four companies put together the final concept paper that served as the basis for structuring the new venture.

The organizing group had hoped to raise as much as $15 million, comparable to Adela's initial capital, and the authorized capital was set at that amount. Unlike the earlier ventures, the founders agreed that all shareholders would own the same number of shares, and they settled on $200,000 per company. Clearly, the founders considered their investment as seed money that would have to be leveraged from other sources at a later date. Specifically, they hoped to reach a cooperative relationship with the United States government in carrying out this concept.

The offering memorandum prepared by the intellectual founders spoke eloquently about the danger of worldwide hunger and depressed conditions in rural areas. It pointed out the growing interest of the United States government in seeking to involve the private sector to deal with these twin problems. It justified participation by other private corporations on both humanitarian grounds as well as en-lightened self-interest.

It argued that smaller investments of less than $1 million would be the most effective way of accomplishing their objectives. The memorandum emphasized that market considerations would dominate investment decisions. Most of the guide-lines set down in the concept paper were in fact incorporated into LAAD's Articles of Incorpora-tion and the company's operating policies.

This narrative provides an historical record of one corporation's experience during a period of historical economic and political transition in Latin America. It offers insights into matters of man-agement, risk assessment, problem solving, as well as of the region's economic development.

A basic philosophical and operating tenet of LAAD has been its emphasis on people, which explains why specific names of persons appear frequently in the text. Corporations and institu-tions do not make things happen. People do.

1

Poverty and the Cold War

At the time LAAD was created, the world was caught in the middle of the Cold War. The United States was fighting in Vietnam, the Prague Spring had polarized the two superpowers, and the East-West conflict over the loyalties of the Third World was in full swing. Latin America was prominently displayed on the battlefield screens of the cold warriors with Fidel Castro consolidated in Cuba and actively supporting guerilla and other leftist movements throughout the region.

The United States government was supporting reformist movements under the aegis of the Alliance for Progress. This policy initiative designed to help friendly Latin American countries introduce social reforms was intended to address such perceived problems as unfair land ownership, tax structures, and basic human needs. Many Latin American governments at the time were in the hands of dictators or the military, some reformist, some not. A Socialist-Communist alliance had just taken power democratically in Chile. In this scenario, the United States had no secure allies. Everything appeared up for grabs.

Many policymakers in the United States attributed the social unrest in Latin America to the wide gap in income and wealth between the rich and poor. These policymakers were the authors of the Alliance for Progress, by then already ten years old. Many of their arguments had been drawn from the controversial Argentine economist Raul Prebisch, my former boss. A one-time president of the Argentine Central Bank, he became world famous after his appointment as executive secretary of the Latin American Economic Commission for Latin America (ECLA). Dr. Prebisch used his new visibility to develop his "structuralist" interpretation of Latin America's comparatively low living standard and slow rate of growth. This structuralist approach evolved during the 1950s and took center stage among the development economists by the end of that decade.

Dr. Prebisch argued that Latin America depended too much on the export of a few commodities, whose prices were falling relative to the prices of imported industrial goods. His solution for that was to encourage national import substitution, particularly of industrial goods, and economic integration to promote regional import substitution in those industries with large economies of scale.

Second, he argued that the state should play a leading role in developing critical or strategic industries and public utilities. He encouraged centralized economic planning to consolidate the state's leading role in economic development. He backed exchange controls as a mechanism for channeling scarce hard currency to priority purposes. He urged tax reform to redistribute the tax burden to the wealthier taxpayers.

In agriculture, he argued that stagnating agricultural production was caused by extreme

inequality in land ownership, which made it impossible for the poorest farmers to produce, because they lacked the land. He contrasted them
with the wealthy *"latifundistas,"* who already
earned enough money to live and lacked the
incentive to increase output on their extensive holdings.

These theories found fertile ground among the
political left, because it gave them an intellectual
argument to attack their traditional conservative
enemies and to criticize the United States. The
military and political nationalists were attracted to
the leading role of the state, since they had already embarked on state capitalism in such countries as Argentina, Brazil, and Chile. In some countries, the military actually made common cause
with leftists. Just about everyone at the time op-
posed the International Monetary Fund, whose mission was to encourage stable exchange rates as
part of a world trading order. The IMF typically
proposed fiscal austerity to restore investor confidence and to meet international obligations. Open
verbal clashes between supporters and detractors
of the IMF were as much a daily event back then
as they are today, although the IMF's detractors
today are no longer just on the left.

Dr. Prebisch's arguments were thoroughly debated in Washington. In a masterful move designed
to take the moral high ground away from the Cuban approach to development, President John F.
Kennedy announced the Alliance for Progress in
1961. This new policy committed the United States
to promote economic and social reform throughout Latin America and to a major increase in foreign economic assistance for the region.

Generous aid programs directly from the U.S. Agency for International Development and indirectly through international development institutions funneled billions of dollars into the region.

Reformist arguments were the order of the day. Agrarian reform took center stage and was openly supported and even financed by AID. Meanwhile, agricultural production inside Latin America was stagnating, partially because of the political uncertainties surrounding agriculture and land ownership, and partly because reformist governments often controlled the prices of basic foods to keep the lid on popular discontent in urban areas.

The vast bulk of this financial assistance was channeled to the public sector. Some U.S. government officials considered the private sector in Latin America with some hostility, blaming it for benefiting the rich and for underwriting right-wing dictatorships. Consequently, the private sector received only a tiny percentage of the total funding channeled to the region.

It is clear that the primary motivation for this massive aid program to Latin America was intended to stem the spread of Communist influence and to strengthen the overall security position of the United States and its allies. Many years later, after the Berlin Wall was dismantled and the threat of Communism evaporated, U.S. aid to Latin America evaporated and aid flows from America's allies soon followed suit.

American corporations active in Latin America generally supported these aid efforts at the time. Some put their own money and executive time into efforts designed to strengthen private enterprise in the region. The largest of these private initiatives was Adela. Another was the International Basic Economy Corporation funded by the Rockefeller family, which focused on capital markets, supermarkets, poultry, and low-cost housing. All of them were designed to bring to bear the creativity and risk taking of private enterprise to accelerate investment in productive assets in Latin America and hence reduce the incidence of poverty.

The motivation behind these initiatives was quite different from today's investment funds specializing in Latin America. The motivation matched the concerns of the day. Although intended to be profitable, the earlier initiatives were more concerned with economic and social progress in Latin America. Their initial impetus was more political than financial. Poverty alleviation was the bottom line for these new private initiatives.

In contrast, today's investment funds operate not in the Third World, but rather in "emerging markets." The countries are the same; the times and themes are not.

Ten years elapsed between the time of President Kennedy's speech on the Alliance for Progress and the formation of LAAD. During that period, vast amounts of resources had been transferred to Latin America, some of which produced long-term benefits. In the agricultural sector, the picture was less encouraging. Agrarian reforms were introduced in Chile, El Salvador and Peru. Bolivia was trying to consolidate its own agrarian reform carried out earlier. In all four countries, agricultural production stagnated as efficient farmers were chased off their land and replaced by poor and inefficient farmers. These new farmers were accustomed to produce for their own families and not for the market place. They were not bankable. They were illiterate and unable to learn new technologies. They received little technical and financial help from their political sponsors and productivity plummeted.

Politicians regarded agriculture as a social, and therefore political, problem. They concerned themselves with the visible inequalities in rural communities Taking from the rich and giving to the poor was the apparent solution. They concerned themselves little with production, and not at all about markets. They assumed that agriculture was a stagnant activity designed to produce basic necessities for the local market or to export traditional commodities to unreliable international markets. The new economic model even discouraged commodity exports, which were frequently taxed. In this way, governments taxed the wealthy and reduced their dependence on traditional exports at a time when government funds were being used to encourage import substitution industries with higher value added.

The political motivations were well intentioned, but the unintended result of these actions was to discourage investment in agriculture and production not only stagnated, but it actually fell in many countries.

By the time LAAD was proposed, a growing number of business executives and U.S. government officials were looking for new ways of energizing agriculture through private enterprise. The need was clearly felt, but concrete initiatives were still few and far between. The stage was set.

2

An Idea is Born

The company was incorporated in Panama on January 26 , 1970. Panama was chosen because of its location inside Latin America and because its government does not tax income from business conducted outside of its borders. The company was named the Latin American Agribusiness Development Corporation. Neither this name, nor its acronym, LAAD, won any accolades on Madison Avenue. What the name lost in elegance, it gained in clarity of purpose.

Twelve corporations were named in the original registration. At $200,000 apiece, LAAD's initial paid-in capital came to $2.4 million.

The Articles of Incorporation gave each shareholder the right to appoint one director to the board. Certain restrictions were added to those Articles, such as a right of first refusal on the sale of shares to new stockholders, designed to insure the philosophical integrity of the company over the long term. This restriction proved its value many years later when the right was exercised to prevent the sale of LAAD shares to corporations which did not share the developmental mission of the company.

The policy of equal ownership proved to be one of the glues that kept the shareholders together through good times and bad. No one was particularly unhappy during the bad times and no one benefited unduly in the good ones. It encouraged a sense of camaraderie among the directors which was critical to maintaining shareholder interest in an activity not directly related to their business.

Once the company was formed, the first board meetings discussed operating priorities. Although there was a philosophical accord among the shareholders, disagreements emerged in the board of directors over operations. Some directors felt that LAAD should primarily provide technical assistance, drawing on its shareholders for the necessary know-how. That view had some merit in light of LAAD's limited financial resources, but the majority decided to provide financing to worthwhile agribusiness projects as the main thrust. This decision was important, because it would eventually allow LAAD to earn sufficient profits from operations to reinvest in future growth and to raise money from other lending institutions.

The company proceeded to open a tiny office in the back room of a New York City cosmetics firm on Fifth Avenue and set out to make its mark in the world. Fred Orth became the company's first interim president. He was backed up by a retired Bank of America officer, August Maffrey, while the bank itself temporarily provided accounting and other support services.

Funding was the first order of business. The company's $2.4 million of paid-in capital was woefully inadequate to accomplish its goals LAAD sought funding from the United States government in hopes of building a public-private partnership to fund agribusiness investments in rural Latin America. This concept was very much in the minds of the founders, because such a partnership gave greater credence to the developmental thrust of the company. The founders also thought this would benefit LAAD's public image.

The company first approached the Overseas Private Investment Corporation (OPIC), a U.S. government-funded corporation providing political risk insurance and loans to support private American investment in the Third World. The logic of an OPIC-LAAD partnership was there, but OPIC required 95 percent beneficial American ownership of all its clients incorporated overseas. Since LAAD was incorporated in Panama and had one European shareholder (Adela), it did not qualify for OPIC funding.

LAAD also approached the International Finance Corporation (IFC). The IFC turned LAAD down because of its lack of experience. Also, IFC's lending rates were similar to those that LAAD expected to charge its clients in Latin America.

The critical breakthrough occurred when one of LAAD's directors, Don Kirchhoff, president of the Standard Fruit and Steamship Company (now the Dole Food Company), put the company in touch with Thomas Mooney in Guatemala. Tom had recently left Adela as its regional investment officer for Central America and was trying to set up a private investment company for that region. He was credited with having successfully built a portfolio of joint ventures and loans while with Adela.

He lacked the capital to launch his idea, but had made progress convincing the AID about the feasibility of his idea. AID had informally offered Tom a long term loan for use in Central America on condition that he raise risk capital from American corporations and banks.

Tom met with LAAD's recently appointed president, James Halom, a former executive from the W.R Grace & Company. Both men recognized the logic of merging their two undertakings and agreed to make a joint presentation to AID for funding. Tom knew AID's many requirements, having previously worked for AID in Central America. One of his better known achievements while at AID was setting up a network of locally owned private development finance companies throughout Central America backed by long term concessional loans from AID.

The two men set out to negotiate a $6 million loan from AID through its regional office for Central America—ROCAP. Both sides agreed on concessional terms to help LAAD build its equity base. These terms provided for a twenty-year repayment period, including five years of grace on principal, at an interest rate of 3 percent. Similar terms to these had already been extended to other Central American development finance companies. AID's motivation was institution building in support of LAAD, on the one hand, as well as seeking more efficient ways of channeling needed funding into private enterprise in Central America. LAAD's emphasis on agribusiness development was particularly attractive to AID, because no other AID borrower had offered to focus on this high risk sector. The timing was right for both AID and LAAD.

One stumbling block in the negotiations was how to guarantee the loan. AID had requested a corporate guarantee from LAAD's shareholders, but they were not willing to increase their exposure in LAAD at that time. The negotiators agreed that LAAD would capitalize a Central American subsidiary, LAAD de Centroamerica S.A. with $2 million, which provided a strong equity base to service the AID loan. In addition, AID placed tight restrictions on the type of projects to be financed; prohibited the use of AID funds for projects in which any of LAAD's shareholders had a financial interest; placed a 9 percent ceiling on the interest rate LAAD could charge its clients, and controlled the subsidiary's ability to pay dividends to LAAD, as well as LAAD's ability to pay dividends to its shareholders.

Although the terms of the loan were agreed upon in Central America, there remained some opposition to the proposal in AID Washington. Some AID staff members objected to providing concessional funding to a company owned by large multinational corporations. The senior man in AID for Latin American development at the time was Frank Kimball. He had known Tom Mooney for some years and had confidence in his ability to perform. Mr. Kimball was instrumental in persuading his colleagues, but there was a lot of good faith and personal reputations on the table when the actual loan agreement was signed in the summer of 1971.

It was the signing of the loan agreement between LAAD and AID that truly launched the company. A financial institution with only $2.4 million in resources would quickly consume this capital in operating expenses. It is questionable whether LAAD would have survived without AID's financial support at this critical juncture. AID provided both the tenor, the leverage and an interest rate, which made it possible for LAAD to operate profitably. The public-private partnership outlined in LAAD's original concept paper was now a reality.

At the time, it was not possible for LAAD to borrow money from the international capital markets given the high anticipated risk associated with Latin America and the company's lack of operating experience. LAAD had no choice but to seek an alliance with the public sector.

As attractive as AID's terms were to LAAD, that was still no guarantee of success. There are many examples of private development companies that had received similar terms from AID and then failed. The underlying risk of investing in Latin America is evidenced by the number of bankruptcies in the financial arena. The challenge remained daunting, but LAAD now had the kind of resources it needed to prove the feasibility of its concept.

LAAD's relationship with AID was precisely what the founding shareholders had intended— LAAD working in harmony with the public sector in pursuit of common goals. In this case, the partnership was to continue for many years. The original AID loan was for $6 million, but the company signed five subsequent agreements for a total of nearly $50 million for use in both Central America and the Caribbean. We will pick up the AID story later.

By the end of 1971, LAAD had satisfied AID's conditions prior to disbursement and was ready to do business. All beginnings are difficult, and LAAD's was no exception. Tom Mooney was LAAD's greatest asset. He knew both the development business, the region's business community and the region itself. He spoke Spanish and was a good negotiator.

The choice of Central America was fortuitous in many ways. It allowed LAAD to concentrate its efforts in a small geographic area, which was cost effective. We were able to operate initially in five countries with only one field office. Distances were short. The company was able to operate profitably with a small portfolio thanks to its low overhead.

LAAD was less fortunate in developing a viable business with its newly opened Mexico City office, run by Bruce Berckmans. Bruce was an American, who lived many years in Mexico, spoke Spanish, and had many local contacts. Unfortunately, the Central American operation had preempted all of LAAD's available capital. We tried to keep the Mexican operation going by selling technical services, but this proved insufficient to sustain the office and we reluctantly closed it down in 1973. LAAD lacked the resources to sustain an unprofitable operation for more than a few months.

No thought was given to operating in any other country at the time as LAAD barely had sufficient financial resources to sustain the Central American initiative.

The company in 1971 was a year and a half old; it had the resources necessary to build a viable business based in Central America and its operating policies were in place. The time had come to fish or cut bait.

3

The Players

A central thesis of this book is the role played by people—the key people. The best-structured institution will eventually fail if those directing and managing it are incompetent. Most private companies have three key groups of players: the shareholders, the directors, and the managers. The shareholders put up the capital and determine the mission of the venture; the directors set the policy to carry out the mission and oversee management's performance, while management carries out board policies, manages the work force and deals with day-to-day operational matters. In LAAD's case, we have to add a fourth group, its clients. As a development corporation, LAAD cares about what its clients do with its funding.

The Shareholders

LAAD's shareholders are all multinational agribusiness and financial corporations. These were the players who proposed and capitalized the company in the first place. They determined our mission and business philosophy.

They decided that LAAD would be a development corporation focusing on agribusiness in Latin America. As players in an international ideological struggle that could affect their overall business interests, these corporations felt that they should make common cause with the local business community by helping them build new productive assets and become more profitable. A country which fosters local private investment typically offers more acceptable rules of the game to foreign investors. Therefore, LAAD would give preference in its financing activities to countries which offered nondiscriminatory, clear rules of the game. LAAD would only finance privately owned and managed companies. It would not support state enterprises, even if the company could make money doing so.

It was important to the shareholders that LAAD support small and medium-sized clients, rather than large, well-established businesses. We were encouraged to make smaller loans and investments. Over the years, the average size of LAAD's loans fluctuated around $300,000, with little upward trend, despite inflation and the growth in the company's ability to make larger loans.

The shareholders helped identify potential clients and offered technical and marketing advice. The Dole Food Company provided help with banana growers in Ecuador, Costa Rica and Honduras; grapefruit growers in Honduras and pineapple farmers in Costa Rica. Ralston Purina assisted us with shrimp farmers in Peru and Venezuela, and a hog farmer in Mexico. Cargill helped us understand the market risk associated with LAAD's large exposure to the citrus industry in Belize and the coffee industry in general. Goodyear advised us on the rubber industry.

Whenever we explored the possibility of starting operations in a new country, our shareholders would put us in touch with their business contacts and associates. When first setting foot in a new market, the first people on our list to visit were always the local managers of our shareholders.

From the beginning, the shareholders considered themselves as equal partners in this venture and the articles of incorporation were written in such a way as to encourage each of them to own exactly forty shares of common stock.

The shareholders drafted the articles of incorporation to preserve their control over the company. Not only did the founding shareholders each purchase the same number of shares of common stock, but all new shareholders followed suit. The shareholders wanted to limit ownership in the company to those corporations which shared LAAD's development objectives. In particular, they wanted to exclude shareholders mainly interested in earning a profit from their investment. Article III gives LAAD a right of first refusal on the sale of any outstanding shares to new stockholders and, for good measure, the shareholders themselves retained an additional right of first refusal even if the company declined to exercise it. These provisions provided long term continuity in policy by limiting the shareholder group to companies with common goals. Continuity of purpose was one of the key reasons for LAAD's long term impact and viability. Consequently, LAAD's original mission remains as valid today as it did in 1969.

The shareholders agreed that LAAD should be a profit-making corporation, but that profits were not the primary motive for creating the company. This philosophy was repeatedly upheld. The shareholders never pressured the company to maximize profits per se nor to increase dividends.

From the shareholders' perspective, LAAD was not considered part of their core business activities, even though it was intended to be a profitable venture. LAAD's earnings could not even be consolidated into their financial statements, because individual ownership in the company never exceeded 20 percent, the minimum percentage needed to use the equity method of accounting.

The shareholders were always concerned about LAAD's public image. Whereas profits were not a primary goal, image was. Anything that might cast a poor image on LAAD could reflect on the shareholders themselves. Thus, the company was never allowed to finance projects involving alcohol for human consumption or tobacco for cigarettes; it avoided financing projects owned by prominent politicians; and it was very careful to avoid businesses whose owners might be involved in other illegal or even questionable activities.

The international name recognition of our shareholders proved to be an intangible asset to LAAD in that it gave the company a stature and importance well beyond its financial strength and small size. It facilitated LAAD's access to senior government officials and commercial bankers. It helped our investment officers to identify themselves to new clients who had never heard of the company.

One of the more difficult issues for the share-holders to determine was the market value of their investment in LAAD. Its shares have never been openly traded because of the right of first refusal clause. Occasionally, because of restructuring, changing market conditions, or new management, some shareholders expressed a desire to sell their shares. There has never been an easy way of selling these shares and no market price to determine value. Consequently, those shareholders would look to LAAD to redeem the shares.

In 1988, three shareholders indicated their desire to sell their shares back to the company. After a very long debate, it was decided to authorize LAAD to repurchase the shares over a three-year period at their original par value. The prevailing argument was that profit had not been the prime motivation behind the original investment in LAAD and, therefore, no shareholder should profit from selling out. This policy also clearly discouraged the other shareholders from doing the same.

LAAD's legal structure provided long term stability in ownership and continuity in policy direction. LAAD's shares were never traded on the open market, which has made it impossible to fix a market value for its shares. The only practical way to establish a market value would be to quote LAAD's common shares on a stock exchange. This issue was discussed by the shareholders, but they always preferred to maintain full ownership in order to perserve LAAD's developmental mission.

The Directors

With forty shares of common stock, each shareholder has the right to appoint one director. With twelve shareholders, a typical board meeting would consist of nine or ten directors, a manageable number. There are enough directors to allow a meaningful debate with opposing views but not so many that speeches substitute discourse. LAAD's board has never been a rubber stamp body. Issues have always been thoroughly debated and decisions taken.

Like most boards, LAAD's directors provide policy guidance, review corporate and individual performance, and oversee operations. A loan and investment committee reviews all equity proposals regardless of size as well as all loans above management's discretionary limit, currently set at $500,000. The audit committee analyzes the audited financial statements and focuses particularly on the adequacy of the reserves against possible losses. The compensation committee controls the compensation of all senior executives.

As a board, the directors behave similarly to their counterparts in large companies throughout the United States. Because they represent large multinational corporations, the directors have always insisted that LAAD comply with all rules governing large corporations, including ethical behavior, compliance with standard American accounting principles, following commercial bank loan classifications, and disclosing information on the company periodically to the public through printed annual reports.

To encourage broad participation by the directors, the positions of chairman and vice chairman are rotated every two years as are the chairmanships and membership of the three board committees.

One major contribution of the directors to LAAD has been their knowledge and experience of doing business in Latin America. LAAD's directors have always been senior executives usually with responsibility for Latin American operations. Most of them had many years of experience in the field. Typically, at least one director would have personal knowledge of the industry and markets for the investment proposals submitted for approval. Management has avoided many potentially bad loans by heeding their advice. The directors themselves often provided contacts and an overview when management was considering entering a new country in addition to the assistance provided by the shareholders through their local managers.

Typically, LAAD's directors were given broad authority to speak for their respective corporations without having to check back with their superiors for guidance or specific instructions. This policy encouraged open debate and prompt decisions.

By far the greatest contribution of the directors was their overall business acumen on a broad range of issues. Directors from agribusiness firms were familiar with markets for agricultural products and business operating problems, while banking directors were sensitive to country exposure and issues of financial management. Management could look to its directors for advice during board meetings as well as outside of them.

In a world of changing priorities and political realities, it is remarkable that successive directors would reaffirm repeatedly the original mission of the Corporation. The directors review the direction and strategy of LAAD every year as management updates a running three-year plan. Although operations policies and the rate of growth in loan activity would be updated to reflect market conditions, at no time did the directors change LAAD's basic mission.

The Managers

All of the management team had business experience in Latin America prior to joining LAAD. However, only a few of them had received an education in agriculture and only one had earned a Ph. D in agricultural economics. Knowledge of the area and of its people took precedence over technical skills in agriculture.

The most valuable asset of LAAD's managers is their ability to judge people (in particular potential clients) and to negotiate an agreement which reflects the risk assessment of the project. LAAD's managers are also called upon to do conventional business analyses of projects, some of which are rejected because they are not considered technically or economically viable. However, few projects get approved based on their technical and financial viability alone. Managers must be able to assess the strengths and weaknesses of the sponsors of the companies that we finance.

LAAD's management structure is a horizontal one. Its business managers are the field representatives who live in one of the countries that they serve. These representatives report directly to one senior executive in the head office, who, in turn,

reports directly to the president. This flat management structure encourages a rapid response from
the head office and quick decisions on making
financial commitments and managing the portfolio. It also keeps operating expenses down. The
company has virtually no staff functions within
management, except for treasury and accounting
services. Specialized staff functions, such as legal
or occasional technical advice, are hired independently or provided by shareholders.

Field managers are responsible for identifying
projects, structuring them, analyzing them, writing the internal investment proposal, defending the
project before whomever has the final decision,
closing the deal once it is approved, making certain that all conditions prior to disbursement are
met, and working with the client until the loan is
paid back or the equity investment sold. The country manager is supported by one administrative
assistant.

One difficult decision when selecting resident
managers has always been whether to choose an
expatriate or hire a national professional. We have
concluded that "knowledge of whom" outweighs
the "knowledge of what." This led us to chose
professionals who are citizens of the country where
they reside or are married to a citizen of that country. Not only do the nationals do a better job of
choosing the right clients, they are better equipped
to solve local problems. Hiring local talent also
implies much lower operating expenses, because
an expatriate can easily cost double the cost of a
comparable national professional. The expatriate
will typically request a range of benefits, such as
home leave, housing allowance, cost of living dif-

ferential, and an educational allowance, in addition to a higher salary. The primary reason for choosing a national, however, is performance, not expenses.

To date, we have given preference to nationals who have been educated in American universities, partly because of their knowledge of English and partly because they generally have a more international outlook. Hopefully, as Latin American universities improve their curricula, we will rely more on them for future hirings.

Finally, all of LAAD's senior management has been brought up from within the organization. No senior officer has ever been hired from outside the company.

The current president of the company, Benjamin Fernandez, started with the company in 1976. Ben was born in Cuba but raised in Asturias, Spain before emigrating to the United States as a teenager. He studied accounting at Florida International University and was a member of that university's first graduating class. A former Price Waterhouse auditor, he started as an accountant and quickly rose to financial analyst, vice president, and executive vice president, before taking the top position. He earned his wings during the difficult years in the 1980s when he was called upon to face numerous problem clients. Ben learned how to assess difficult situations and come up with workable solutions. He stays focused on key issues until they are resolved to his satisfaction.

The treasurer, Oscar Alvarez, has been with LAAD since 1979 and also started as an accountant. He too was born in Cuba and was educated there under the Communist system until he emigrated to the United States as a teenager. He also graduated with Ben in accounting from Florida International University in its first class. At LAAD, he rose to comptroller and gradually took over all of the financial management of the company. He became treasurer and vice president around the time LAAD began to tap the international markets for medium term financing. He had to persuade skittish banks that LAAD was a better credit risk than Latin America and he succeeded. Gifted with a prodigious memory, he could explain to his bankers how LAAD had proven its ability to solve problems in even the most difficult of circumstances, thereby warranting more favorable treatment than would otherwise have been the case given LAAD's exposure to Latin American risk.

The regional vice presidents, J. Hunter Martin and Carlos Julio Ravelo, have been with the company for fifteen and twelve years respectively, both starting as country managers.

Hunter was an English major at the University of Virginia. He then earned an MBA from the University of Southern California which led to a position with the Standard Fruit Company (one of LAAD's shareholders) in Central America. When he joined LAAD, he was sent to open its office in Barbados with the impossible task of developing a portfolio of agribusiness loans in the small Caribbean islands where agriculture was slowly dying. After a brief stint in the Dominican Republic, he went to head up LAAD's office in San Jose, Costa Rica. Always the gentleman and diplomat, Hunter quickly earned the respect of his clients in that region.

Carlos Julio was born in the Dominican Republic and went off to study agriculture at Texas A&M University where he continued his studies until earning a doctorate degree in agricultural economics. Like Hunter, he also was hired by the Standard Fruit Company in Central America and in Ecuador. Carlos Julio is the best negotiator among the LAAD executives and he has proven effective at building up a loan portfolio in new countries.

Both men distinguished themselves by managing their portfolios during the difficult years and gradually assumed responsibility for other countries and LAAD offices. After years of strong performance in the field, they were elected regional vice presidents and moved to Coral Gables during the 1990s.

All of LAAD's senior executives learned most of their knowledge on the job, building the business and solving problems. The company complemented this experience by investing heavily in specialized courses, including the Harvard Business School (advanced international management), Stanford University (strategic planning), INSEAD, France (international financial management), the University of Virginia Dardens School (management) and INCAE, Costa Rica (financial analysis). We also took advantage of specialized training offered by our shareholders, such as Bank of America (credit analysis) and Cargill (management style).

None of this training was available to those who chose to work for an undercapitalized company in the early 1970s. If one man can be credited with that job, it was Thomas Mooney, the man who negotiated LAAD's first AID loan and in charge of the company's only operating office, then in

Guatemala. Tom was born in St. Louis, Missouri and might still be living there had not World War II found him parachuting out of an American troop carrier behind Japanese lines in mainland China. If nothing else, this experience taught him the art and rewards of survival. After the war, he held several U.S. government jobs before joining the World Bank, which decided to use his talents in Central America. There, he married a Guatemalan lady and settled down.

Following the World Bank, he worked for many years with AID where he successfully pioneered the concept of using AID money to provide long term concessional loans to local development finance companies capitalized by local businessmen. This became a popular program that was repeated in many other Latin American countries. In the process of creating these new companies, he traveled throughout the region meeting businessmen who eventually formed a loose network of contacts for him.

After AID, he was hired by Adela, where he pioneered the idea of investing in new ventures with three more or less equal partners: a local partner able to provide local management and contacts; a foreign partner bringing technology and access to markets; and Adela, the financial partner and arbitrator in case of disagreement between the first two. This formula was repeatedly applied in Central America, making it one of Adela's few profitable regions.

After leaving Adela, he tried to set up his own development finance company with private American capital and long term AID funding, using the same concept he had introduced many years before. When he eventually merged his own initiative with LAAD, he managed the company's Central American subsidiary until his retirement in 1990.

Tom needed all of his survival abilities to get LAAD up off the ground. Not only did he have to develop a portfolio of loans and quasi equity investments meeting LAAD's business requirements, he also had to choose projects that met the various developmental objectives that AID expected LAAD to carry out. This was a tough challenge, because AID's own objectives would shift periodically depending on the mood of its boss, the American Congress. The Japanese may have forced him to learn survival skills, but his patience in dealing with AID was more likely learned from the Chinese.

The Clients

The purpose of any business is to provide a competitive service or product to its customers, and even a development corporation like LAAD is no exception. The company's motives may be unusual for the industry, but the client is only interested in the quality and cost of the service that he receives. LAAD has to compete with other private and public companies in order to build its loan portfolio.

As in the case of any financial institution, LAAD's long-term success is tied to the ongoing success of its clients; only a successful client meets his financial obligations. Also, it is the client who contributes to the economic and social well being of his country, which is the heart of LAAD's mission statement. It is he who creates the new jobs, generates the hard currency, and builds a viable business. LAAD only provides him the means. When we say that LAAD has generated so many jobs or so much hard currency, we are really referring to the accomplishments of our clients. LAAD's main role is carefully selecting the projects and clients who will make the highest contribution to their countries' economy and well being.

Selecting a good client is the most important function of any development or financial institution. It is the clients who repay loans, not the "projects." Projects are euphemisms for the purpose of a loan or equity investment. They can be fixed assets like a fruit orchard or a processing plant, or sometimes working capital to make a fixed asset produce what it was designed to do. To date, LAAD has financed some 700 projects, but in each case one person or group of persons was responsible for that project.

Successful projects are managed by successful people. An analysis of our portfolio clearly demonstrates the importance of those people. Regrettably, some of our projects failed to achieve their objectives and went out of business. With the exception of the Sandinista debacle in Nicaragua, virtually all project failure can be attributed to human failure. Competent businessmen anticipate risk and manage it.

Droughts, floods, hurricanes, volcanic eruptions, and other natural disasters will always cause havoc in agriculture, but none of our clients went bankrupt because of them. Market prices often fall far below the level projected in our internal project assessments and cause cyclical losses, but they cause consolidation, not failure, in a well managed company. Insects, fungae, rot, and other harmful pathogens can cause extensive crop damage and run up the cost of controlling them with chemicals or other means, but they are all a cost of business to be managed.

Nothing, but nothing, will protect a business from an incompetent or dishonest owner. Our only protection is to avoid funding him in the first place. Of course, we always seek adequate collateral for our loans, but most bad loans lose money regardless of the amount of collateral.

During LAAD's first thirty years, the average write-off per year on its agribusiness loan portfolio has been under seven tenths of one percent, which demonstrates that lending to agriculture in emerging markets can be a viable business, provided you carefully select your clients.

Fortunately for LAAD, we have found that our most reliable borrowers have been the small and medium sized local entrepreneur targeted by our shareholders at the outset.

Before we enter a country for the first time, we try to assess the mental attitude of our potential clients before entering into any loan negotiations. On several occasions, we postponed entering a particular markets precisely because we felt uncomfortable with the way local businessmen think. A lack of interest in production costs, disdain for accounting numbers, absence of a marketing plan are all symptomatic of an attitude problem and a sufficient reason to stay out of that country. Many times, these attitudes are holdovers from a different economic order prevailing in the recent past.

Eventually, the market place will force business-men with an attitude problem to toe the line, but until that moment arrives, LAAD is better off staying out of that particular country, even when the overall investment conditions may otherwise be attractive.

4

The Game Begins

With its paid-in capital of $2.4 million and a signed $6 million loan from AID, the moment of truth had arrived. It would be nice to say that LAAD set out to execute a well-prepared business strategy with a detailed market study, but the reality was quite different. No one was lining up at our doorstep for funding. Tom had to look for projects much like a clam digger when the tide is low on the Chesapeake Bay, by painstaking patience and looking for telltale signs. We were not the only lender on the block; other clam diggers were searching with buckets of money in hand. Although the local banking system rarely ventured into the business of project financing, there were other AID funded development finance companies also offering medium term funding in dollars throughout Central America. Their terms were similar to LAAD's. Fortunately for us, they proved less inclined to finance agriculture because of its perceived high risk.

In May of 1972, the Board of Directors offered me the job of president. The directors were concerned that the company was not making enough progress in generating new business and was looking for new leadership. For me, this represented a unique opportunity to build something from nothing and I quickly accepted, although the future of the company was far from assured.

Fortunately, I knew Tom before from our Adela days and we were able to work together well as a team. I gave him free reign to develop project opportunities and Tom was a man who appreciated independence.

We made the usual rounds of government development banks and official investment promotion offices, but these visits yielded little of lasting value. Projects recommended by them turned out to be substandard. They were often on the verge of bankruptcy, owned by favored politicians, hopelessly under capitalized, over dimensioned or poorly managed. These visits were politically necessary, but not productive. Only in Nicaragua did we have any success using a local government agency, INFONAC, as a source of project leads.

There proved to be no substitute for beating the bushes in person. We never knew from where the next project might come. While landing at the San Jose, Costa Rica airport one day, Tom noticed a flower farm at the end of the runway. Once he had passed through customs, he took a taxi to the farm and inquired about the owner. Being a small farm, it did not take long for Michael Thomas, the American farm owner, to appear. Mr. Thomas had brought his family to Costa Rica two years earlier.

A flower grower in Florida, he invested all of his savings in his new farm. However, like many pioneers, he lacked the working capital to see himself through the difficult first years. When Tom arrived unannounced on the scene, Mr. Thomas was struggling to build his farm. His need for working capital on the one hand and Tom's need to disburse funds led to a quick agreement and to a relationship that continues to this day.

Mr. Thomas not only survived, he prospered and became the largest single flower grower in the region. An example of successful entrepreneurship, he indirectly encouraged many other American and Costa Rican farmers to grow flowers, leatherleaf fern and ornamental plants. His company, the American Flower Corporation, is one of Costa Rica's largest floriculture enterprises and the day-to-day management of the company is now in the hands of his four sons. LAAD financed most of the Thomas' expansion into carnations in Cartago, leatherleaf fern on the Poas volcano, a macadamia farm and processing plant in Siquirres and a fern farm in Panama.

Floriculture is today Costa Rica's largest non-traditional agricultural export and is a major employer of people in rural areas particularly in the highlands. The fact that Costa Rica has emphasized the cultivation of cut flowers and ornamental plants can be traced more to Mr. Thomas' move to that country than to any official promotional efforts.

Mr. Thomas not only had to learn how to grow flowers efficiently in a different environment than Florida, he also had to solve many problems inherent in start-up operations. He had to convince the airlines to offer cargo space from San Jose to Miami. This service did not exist at the time he arrived, but it was critical if his flowers were to have sufficient shelf life once they arrived in Miami. Initially he had to ship his flowers through Panama with its superior air service, but eventually he was able to obtain direct service out of San Jose. Today, floral products are the largest single agricultural export by air cargo from Costa Rica.

In Panama, Tom found a medium-sized Panamanian poultry farmer, Arturo Don Melo. Like Mr. Thomas, this was entirely a family affair. He, too, lacked the capital necessary to build his business, which required considerable vertical integration to be successful in a competitive market. We first financed an egg hatchery, but over the years we financed his broiler operations, a feed mill, a warehouse, a slaughterhouse, and working capital to help him recover from the damage wrought by the American invasion of his country. He is now Panama's largest poultry producer with plans to export poultry products, a first for that country. Mr. Melo remains today one of LAAD's most important clients in that country. Day-to-day management has been gradually assumed by his children.

In Guatemala, the country where LAAD has financed the largest number of projects, we funded the country's first vegetable freezing plant, Alimentos Centroamericanos (ALCOSA), originally designed to sell to the Central American market. Unfortunately, there were few freezers in the region to hold the frozen vegetables either in the supermarkets or in the homes, and the project did not prosper.

At about this time, an American company, Hanover Brands, was well advanced in testing the growing of certain vegetables in the Guatemalan highlands with the idea of freezing them and exporting them to its on-going business in Pennsylvania. Hanover bought out ALCOSA and LAAD provided an additional loan to expand and modernize the plant to meet U.S. standards.

The company became a remarkable success not only for its owners, but also for the country, and particularly for the Indian farmers living in the highlands. ALCOSA provided seed, agricultural inputs, technical assistance and a guaranteed market to the Indians, some of whom had already sold fresh vegetables on the local market while others eked out an existence growing corn. ALCOSA specialized in freezing cauliflower, broccoli, and brussels sprouts, all for the U.S. market.

The new product mix increased the income farmers could produce per hectare with major social consequences benefiting their families and neighboring villagers. The higher incomes made it possible for these farmers to hire outside workers. This allowed them to take their children out of the fields and send them to school. The impact of this project was thoroughly studied by a sociologist from American University on contract with AID. For many years, the project became a popular case study at the Harvard Business School on agribusiness management in emerging markets.

Some tensions did develop between ALCOSA and its Indian suppliers, as often happens in the processing industry. Hanover was concerned with meeting its supply commitments in the United States and encouraged the Indians to expand their production. The Indians thought they had a firm commitment to buy whatever they produced. One year, weather conditions were particularly favorable for cauliflower, but the harvest window was reduced substantially by the warm weather. The unexpected leap in production over a shortened harvest period caught the company unprepared. It could not store the cauliflower without losing quality, but its installed capacity was insufficient to handle the flood of product. The company decided not to buy the entire production, which they were not obliged to under the contract. The company pointed to the contract, while the Indians argued they were verbally assured the company would stand by them. This caused considerable suffering to some of the communities and there was concern that the Indians would turn their back on the company in future years.

As a precaution against a repetition of that experience, the company put in another production line and prepared itself to sell any surplus production to the U.S. fresh market. The following year was more successful and the business not only survived but prospered. Within a few years a half dozen new vegetable freezing plants were built copying the ALCOSA model, several of them being financed by LAAD. These new plants provided competition to ALCOSA, thereby affording the Indians a choice. Today, frozen vegetables are one of Guatemala's major agricultural exports and one that generates thousands of rural jobs for both men and women.

One day, Tom noticed mushrooms on display at a Guatemalan supermarket. The store manager told him that they were grown locally by Alfonso Novales. Tom contacted Mr. Novales and learned that he needed funds to expand his business and was unable to obtain credit from local banks. Mr. Novales knew little about growing mushrooms but he had obtained useful information from U.S. Department of Agriculture brochures. He persuaded LAAD to made him a modest loan. At first, he prospered, but the Guatemalan earthquake of 1976 destroyed his mushroom houses and all of his production. Much of the damage caused by that earthquake took place in rural areas and affected adobe houses. The Guatemalan government, trying to limit damage from future earthquakes, prohibited any further construction of adobe houses. Since Mr. Novales' mushroom houses were made of adobe, he was unable to rebuild and was forced out of business. He repaid his loan to LAAD and later re-entered the business using a different mushroom variety and different facilities. Not every project succeeds, but a persevering entrepreneur can.

In Costa Rica, we entered into a long term relationship with a local family enterprise managed by Miguel Angel Rodriguez, a man who later became a presidential candidate in two national elections and was elected that country's president in 1998. Back in the early 1970s, Mr. Rodriguez, in partnership with Adela, was building an integrated beef business, including slaughterhouses in Costa Rica and Honduras, a cattle ranch along the border with Nicaragua, a tannery in Costa Rica and a marketing subsidiary in the United States. LAAD financed all of the projects located in Central America. The beef industry at that time was growing rapidly based on shipping lean industrial grade beef to the United States and select cuts to Puerto Rico. Central America was one of the few areas in

Latin America free of the hoof and mouth disease. This advantage was critical, because the U.S. Department of Agriculture prohibits the importation of uncooked beef from countries where the disease is endemic. Central America was authorized to ship fresh uncooked beef into the United States, primarily for making ground beef.

Many slaughterhouses were built throughout Central America by various investor groups, eight of which were financed by LAAD. The industry showed great promise for two decades. In later years the industry would go through a consolidation, because the U.S. beef market fell into a prolonged recession resulting from the decline in per capita American beef consumption. Today, only Nicaragua has the potential to build a successful export beef industry, while the other Central American countries have either become self-sufficient or are actually importing beef. Nicaragua is the only country in Central America where LAAD continues to support the beef industry.

In El Salvador, LAAD found a Nicaraguan businessman, Mr. Humberto Mantica, who wanted to build a sesame seed plant. Mr. Mantica already owned a sesame decorticating plant in his home country and had convinced the Salvadoran government to provide working capital to small farmers to grow this labor-intensive crop. LAAD provided a loan to Procesadora Agricola Salvadorena to build the plant, which purchased seed from up to 2,000 small Salvadorean farmers.

One of LAAD's first loans in Nicaragua was to Alimentos Amolonca, a vegetable freezing plant similar to ALCOSA, that was shipping frozen okra and black eyed peas to the Safeway supermarket chain in the United States. Amolonca was a major source of employment in the Chinandega region. The company operated with great promise until the Sandinista takeover in 1979, when it was expropriated by the new government and the business was run into the ground.

The number and diversity of projects quickly multiplied. Within a few years, we had expanded into all of Central America, financing a wide range of projects, including hogs and poultry, flower seeds, floriculture, horticulture, sesame seed, rubber processing, wooden furniture and food distribution.

The vast majority of the projects financed during these initial years were owned and managed by local families. About half of them were new projects and half expansions of existing enterprises. About half of them supplied local markets with the other half selling overseas. This degree of diversification was possible because the region still benefited from a low level of inflation and stable exchange rates.

While Tom was focusing on building up LAAD's project financing business in Central America, I was looking for additional capital. LAAD was originally capitalized with $2.4 million. However, one shareholder, Dow Chemical Company, announced its intention to withdraw even as it purchased its forty shares of LAAD stock. LAAD had to agree to refund Dow's investment over a three-year period.

Meanwhile, LAAD's first portfolio problems surfaced on an unexpected front. During its first pre-operating years, LAAD had borrowed short term bank money to purchase short-term commercial paper issued primarily by private Mexican companies through American brokers. This paper was yielding a razor thin 1 percent gross margin, which it was hoped would strengthen LAAD's early profitability. Unfortunately, two Mexican steel companies in LAAD's portfolio, Campos Hermanos and Aceros Ecatapec, both went into receivership in 1972 forcing the company to place over $600,000 of its assets on non-accrual. Even more serious was the fact that LAAD had little chance of recovering any of that money in the near future. Between Dow's departure and the Mexican defaults, LAAD only had $1.4 million in equity available to fund its recent commitment to AID to capitalize a Central American subsidiary with $2 million.

With the help of our directors, I set out to visit corporate America hoping to find someone who shared LAAD's vision. With more than a little good luck, three American banks and one manufacturer soon signed on; the Chase Manhattan Bank, the First National Bank of Miami, the Girard Bank of Philadelphia and the Goodyear Tire and Rubber Company. LAAD now had the resources to meet its earlier commitment to AID.

At the same time, we tried to recover as much money as possible from the two Mexican steel companies. By then both companies were controlled by steering committee dominated by large American banks. LAAD had no influence on these deliberations, a lesson that taught us to avoid situations in the future when we might end up in a similar predicament.

We had one unexpected break in the case of Campos Hermanos. That company had effectively lost all of its capital and the creditors, including LAAD, were forced to convert their holdings into common stock of the borrower. Not long after that, a Mexican group offered to buy out all of the common stock in cash, but at a very steep discount. The steering committee accepted the offer and recommended it to all the other participants, all of whom accepted, except for LAAD. Our holding was such a small percentage of the total that our refusal of the offer did not undermine the deal. We were subjected to significant pressure, sometimes through our shareholders, but we refused and the deal went through without us.

Once it was consummated, I asked Adela's Mexico City representative, Rafael Morales to arrange a direct meeting between me and the Mexican group. I flew to Mexico City and met with them in a luxurious mansion worth several times LAAD's net worth. I explained that LAAD was willing to remain a small shareholder in the company until it turned around at which time we would like to sell the shares. Instead of accepting this proposal, they unexpectedly asked whether I would be willing to sell the shares now and mentioned a price above my expectations. I quickly accepted and was told to wait for a call from a broker. I returned to my hotel room and had sandwiches sent up to my room waiting for a phone call. In less than two days, I was indeed called by a broker from the Mexican stock exchange who offered the agreed upon price and the deal was closed that same day. LAAD lost barely 10 percent of its $240,000 exposure compared with the 60 percent loss suffered by the other creditors. For once, being a maverick paid off. Being insignificantly small was helpful too.

Having solved one of LAAD's problem loans and raised sufficient capital to meet our AID commitments, I could refocus on the company itself. Tom was able to fund enough projects to draw down the entire AID loan. Total assets had reached the $10 million mark by 1975 and LAAD was able to show a modest profit for the third consecutive year in a row with a growing return (albeit still modest) on its net worth.

The results of the first AID loan were clearly positive. One pleasant surprise was the low level of problem projects we had in those early years. Agriculture and Latin America appeared less risky than we had feared.

The stage was set to grow and to diversify.

5

From Childhood to Adolescence

The Cold War in the mid-seventies showed no signs of abating. The United States was weakened by post-Vietnam doubts about itself. In Latin America, guerilla movements were emboldened by the Communist victory in Vietnam and, with Cuban backing, became even more aggressive. These political uncertainties in the region continued to complicate LAAD's access to the international capital markets for medium term funding.

The U.S. government, on the other hand, was stepping up its efforts in Central America. AID seemed impressed with LAAD's performance, and this opened the door to a possible second AID loan for that region.

AID sent a team of independent consultants from Checchi & Company to Central America to perform an audit of LAAD's performance under the first loan. Checchi wrote an extensive report covering our operations and performance under the first AID loan. This report gave LAAD generally high marks on the choice of projects and operational management, as well as the overall impact of the program on the Central American economy.

The original AID loan agreement committed LAAD to focus on projects that made the agribusiness chain more efficient, that promoted nontraditional agricultural exports and encouraged the development of a Central American capital market. Checchi concluded that LAAD had turned in a strong performance on the first two goals, but was less successful in the third. We generally agreed with these conclusions, although we did try to comply with the third goal. We, in fact, offered shares of our Central American subsidiary to local investors, and one Honduran company actually swapped its shares for ours and appointed a director to the subsidiary's board.

The Honduran director conscientiously carried out his duties as a director, but his company was also a client and there were conflicting loyalties. We subsequently agreed to reverse the swap and that ended our efforts at capital market development. LAAD was not structured to perform this task and it was not one of our stated missions.

Nevertheless, the overall results of the audit were favorable and Checchi gave AID a positive recommendation to consider a second loan for Central America.

The foreign aid priorities in the United States Congress had shifted since the first loan was signed. Now, the Congress was requiring that AID programs give greater priority to helping the poorest of the poor. This was a period when the so-called "trickle down theories" were in disfavor. AID was under pressure to find more direct ways of benefiting the poorer segments, dubbed "the target man." We never understood exactly who this target man was, but fortunately Washington also had trouble figuring it out. The elusiveness of the target left to us the task of defining a project profile that could reasonably fit within the intent of the legislation.

We looked back at our earlier projects and found that they had created significant amounts of rural employment and that some of the processing plants were buying their raw material from small, often Indian, farmers. We, therefore, proposed to emphasize projects that satisfied one of three criteria: labor-intensive farming, such as floriculture or horticulture; processed raw materials produced by small farmers; or channel funds through an intermediary directly to small farmers. After some discussion, AID accepted those criteria.

Before signing any new loan, we had to find a solution for our capital base, which was too small to support a new multimillion dollar loan. AID insisted that we contribute an additional $2 million in capital to the Central American subsidiary, both as a sign of good faith in supporting the program as well as providing a greater security for the repayment of its loan.

We had recently succeeded in attracting four new shareholders thus raising our paid-in capital to $3 million. We also had accumulated $400,000 in retained earnings, but we were still $600,000 short of satisfying AID's capital requirement.

Management requested a capital increase from the shareholders, but not all of them were willing to subscribe additional funds. Had we raised the necessary equity from those willing to invest, the shareholders would no longer have kept their equal ownership in the company, and this feature was considered critical for the long term survival of LAAD. Instead, we decided to create a new class of non-voting, participating preferred shares. These shares would pay a 5 percent dividend and also participate equally in the payment of any future dividend on the Common Shares. This was not an overly attractive investment at the time, because the prime rate exceeded 5 percent, but eleven of the shareholders committed themselves to increase LAAD's capital by $2.1 million, more than enough to cover the capital requirements of the second AID loan. A new $5 million loan was signed in 1975 for use in Central America.

At the same time, we had identified an opportunity to expand our operations geographically into the Caribbean. We carried out a field survey of possible projects in that region and concluded that there was sufficient demand. Checchi, in its report, had expressed doubts about allowing LAAD to diversify before it had consolidated its position in Central America. Despite this recommendation, we decided to press ahead with the diversification, because the timing appeared right. We submitted a new loan proposal to AID for the Caribbean at the same time as we were signing the second loan for Central America.

The United States was as concerned about the Caribbean as it was about Central America. As always, Cuba remained the chief concern. In many ways, we have to thank the Cuban government for implicitly helping us obtain new funds from AID. Without their anti-American rhetoric and policies, we would probably have had a much more difficult task in raising long term funding from AID.

As it was, agriculture qualified as a high priority sector and AID proved receptive to our proposal based on our track record in Central America. AID indicated it would consider extending a $6 million loan exclusively for the Caribbean, but again conditioned it on LAAD capitalizing a new Caribbean subsidiary with still another $2 million.

The new preferred stock issue provided most of the additional capital, but the remaining capital had to come from reinvesting retained earnings during the draw-down period. A third loan agreement, this time for the Caribbean, was signed in 1976 and we incorporated a new subsidiary, LAAD Caribe S.A.

The purpose of the new loan was also to focus on the poorest segments of society. In addition, AID required us to utilize one quarter of its funding in Haiti, the poorest nation in this hemisphere. In exchange, AID authorized us to include Colombia as an eligible country, our first foray into South America.

By the end of 1976, LAAD had expanded its financial resources to $24 million, exactly ten times its original paid-in capital of $2.4 million in 1970. We had financed eighty-six projects and were operating in ten countries. We had opened a new office in Santo Domingo to handle Caribbean operations.

By now, it was clear that LAAD would be managed as a decentralized company, with all business leads, analyses, negotiations, closings and portfolio management being carried out by country managers. We had no central staff functions, except for the minimum requirements of running a company, such as accounting and treasury. We had no staff technical positions and no in-house legal counsel. We could not have afforded them with our modest resources.

In terms of technical knowledge, we found out that our shareholders and even our clients were better sources of technical information than hiring new technical staff. On the legal front, we found it more effective to use local lawyers to handle all of our legal work in the field. They not only drew up the necessary loan and mortgage agreements, but also handled routine negotiations with local authorities on exchange controls or regulatory issues. In the case of clients in serious default we also relied exclusively on local attorneys. LAAD never lost one lawsuit even though it never hired an in-house attorney, nor did it have any American attorney review the texts of agreements drawn up by its Latin American lawyers.

Disbursing the second and third AID loans proved much easier than the first one. AID was sufficiently pleased with the administration of the first loan, that it simplified its own disbursement procedures in all subsequent loans. Although we learned to live with them, the rules imposed on LAAD by AID in terms of paperwork were substantial and absorbed much staff time.

The new project criteria applied to both loan agreements. We therefore focused more on high value crops, requiring more field labor and on processing plants that were both labor intensive at the plant level, and also purchased raw materials from small farmers. Consequently, food processing, floriculture, and horticulture became our main areas of concentration, replacing cattle, beef, and vegetable oils.

Food processing covered a number of agroindustries. One of them was Leche y Derivados, S.A. (Leyde), a struggling start-up dairy company in Honduras based in the coastal port of La Ceiba. Its main competitor was a large government controlled company that enjoyed a near monopoly position and frequent favors from the government. With aggressive marketing and encouragement of small dairy farmers to increase production, Leyde gradually gained market share against the government company. It is today the largest dairy company selling its products throughout the country.

LAAD's commitment to finance projects in Haiti proved easier than we had anticipated although getting paid in that country did not prove so easy. We actually invested more funds in that country than was required by the AID loan agreement. We financed a dozen projects ranging from a fruit and vegetable canning factory in Cap Haitien on the north coast, to a tomato paste plant in Cavaillon in the southern peninsula, an essential oils plant in Les Cayes, and a fresh mango packing plant for export near the capital. Unfortunately, our experience in that country was uneven and we eventually pulled back, keeping just one client there.

Haiti's agriculture is dominated by a large number of tiny landowners, few of whom can show any legal document attesting to their ownership. There is a handful of larger farms, most of them financially unsuccessful. All of the processing plants in that country have no alternative but to purchase their raw material from Haiti's *minifundio*. This greatly complicates the task of bringing the harvest from the field to the plant.

Sometimes, it is possible to see women walking through the front gate of a processing plant with the day's harvest balanced on their heads. Sometimes, a battered truck drives through the same gate with a weary driver delivering crops from literally hundreds of very small farmers. Much of the country's road system is in disrepair so it is miraculous that any production arrives at all. Paying the farmers is a logistical nightmare, since all transactions must be made in cash, often in extremely remote locations, and individual payments may not exceed the equivalent of a couple of dollars.

Product quality is obviously uneven. Local agriculture is about as close as you can get to organic farming in this hemisphere, since the country uses little agricultural chemicals. The primitive state of the country's basic infrastructure, with its frequent power outages, unreliable telephones and potted streets challenges the most competent of managers. The country's rural population is nearly all illiterate, incapable of reading any kind of instructions. LAAD made a serious attempt to build an agribusiness portfolio in that country, but we have concluded that most productive investments in that country will have to wait until the level of education is significantly improved.

Our greatest success turned out to be in the Dominican Republic, where we had opened an office. Some of our first projects there included a sausage factory, a fertilizer mixing plant and a producer of cigar wrapper tobacco. It did not take long, however, to find that fruits and vegetables offered the greatest opportunity as well as the highest impact in that country.

One of our first high impact projects in the Dominican Republic was a frozen vegetable plant, Southland Frozen Foods, an American-owned plant buying green peas, okra, and other vegetables for export. This was a Dominican version of ALCOSA in Guatemala. Like ALCOSA, Southland provided seed, inputs, and technical assistance to farmers, who proved enthusiastic about increasing their income by selling these nontraditional crops. For LAAD, this provided a successful formula of employing large numbers of workers in the processing plant and a practical way of reaching the country's small farmers.

We funded three companies producing pina colada mix from local coconuts and pineapple. This fruit drink was gaining popularity in the United States, and the Dominican Republic became the largest single supplier to the U.S. market. At least one of these producers, Caribex Dominicana, later diversified into other fruit juices and canned vegetables. LAAD, along with the Overseas Private Investment Corporation, provided funding for several expansions of this company.

We supported a small group of experienced Japanese immigrant farmers growing Chinese vegetables near Santiago de los Caballeros for the Chinese restaurant market in the United States. Growing these vegetables in a tropical climate is complicated by insect infestations and these farmers had to grow their vegetables in a difficult physical environment.

We backed a number of flower farms near Jarabacoa, including one headed by a former minister of agriculture from Haiti, Frantz Flambert, who claims he borrowed money from LAAD because our loan officer wore tennis shoes. Mr. Flambert undoubtedly had more substantial reasons for borrowing the money, but it illustrates how our loan officers communicate with our clients who rarely wear a tie or a jacket. This family-run business is still in operation and is managed by his son.

Not all of the new projects prospered. One that did not was a small slaughterhouse in Belize. This plant had been approved for export to the United States, because it had passed the USDA inspection and because the country had no hoof-and-mouth disease in its cattle herd. In a country with limited production alternatives, Belize's ranchers stood to benefit from this new company. This project eventually failed because of an inadequate supply of cattle in that country. We had originally hoped that the borrower would be able to purchase additional cattle in neighboring countries, but this proved illusory.

LAAD took over the collateral, a cattle ranch called Cool Shade, in a negotiation with the owner, a Belizean businessman from the town of San Pedro. We repeatedly tried to sell the ranch, but were never able to fetch an asking price high enough to cover the outstanding balance on the loan. Faced with the prospect of holding an unproductive asset for more years, we decided to rehabilitate an abandoned patch of thirty acres of citrus. Within a few years, we had expanded the planted area to over 200 acres thanks to technical and managerial assistance we received from the Citrus Company of Belize, a client, and one of two citrus processing plants in the country.

We eventually sold the entire farm to the owner of a Kentucky coal company interested in diversifying his business. We sold the farm for the entire amount of the original loan, plus all the money we had invested in the citrus grove as well as all the interest that the original loan would have generated. The new owner continued to expand the acreage devoted to citrus and the farm now has several thousand acres of producing trees and is the largest single citrus grove in the country.

Our favorable experience with citrus in Belize encouraged us to finance other orange and grapefruit growers and LAAD has since became the largest single source of medium term financing for that industry without a single write-off. The citrus industry is now that country's largest export, replacing sugar. LAAD has funded over thirty projects in Belize for $14 million, including citrus, bananas, and shrimp farming.

The diversification into the Caribbean was psychologically important for LAAD, because it meant we were on the way to becoming a Latin American and Caribbean institution; not just a regional Central American company. In fact, for several years, the Dominican Republic became LAAD's largest single market.

The two new AID loans enabled LAAD to continue growing. The agribusiness portfolio grew by 2.5 times during the four year period 1974-78 reaching $18.5 million. Earnings more than tripled to over $500,000. The diversification had proven to be a success, both financially and in terms of entering new markets.

During 1978, a large European bank, the Rabobank Nederland, a Dutch cooperative bank specializing in serving agribusiness, joined the LAAD shareholder group. We welcomed this new member, not so much for the additional equity, but because we felt the bank was making a strategic investment through us in Latin America. Rabobank has since grown internationally to become a global agribusiness bank with offices in all major Latin American countries. It has became a lead provider of medium term funding and financial services to LAAD.

As we neared the end of the seventies, LAAD was growing and diversifying successfully. We were looking forward to continued expansion. However, events beyond our control would soon dampen our optimism.

6

The Real World

Economists are want to project economic or market growth based on the assumption that "other things are equal." This caveat is intended to exclude from their calculations what they call exogenous factors, events which happen outside the control of the writer. LAAD's market in Central America was relatively quiet. During its first seven years of operations, LAAD had always been operating under gray clouds, which threatened to rain, but never did. Political uncertainty was always present in Central America with its guerilla groups and history of violence. Somehow, the region's governments managed to hold the lid on, and insurrection had not deteriorated into civil war or a revolutionary government. We operated free of those major "exogenous" factors.

This scenario changed dramatically in 1979 with the defeat of Nicaraguan President Anastasio Somoza by the Frente Sandinista de Liberacion Nacional (FSLN). The new Sandinista government lost no time in confiscating the available assets of President Somoza and his closest associates. This action was not surprising, since the president had been the focus of their revolt. We had little direct concern, since LAAD never financed any of President Somoza's enterprises nor of his close relatives.

For awhile, we had hoped to work with the Sandinista government by financing private companies willing to help in the reconstruction of their country. However, the new Sandinista government had other priorities and it showed no interest in working with us. More ominously, the FSLN began widening its expropriation list of companies to include most of the private sector and, more to the point, all of the projects that we had financed.

Our concern with the political landscape in Central America was not limited to Nicaragua. In El Salvador, rebel forces had gained control of major portions of the rural areas, where LAAD would normally operate. Farms and their crops were burned, and terrorism was not limited to the wealthy alone. Many companies shut down, not only because of direct terrorism, but because of a disruption in government services and a growing emigration of Salvadorans abroad. Guatemala also faced a near civil war between the army and a well-armed leftist guerilla force. Honduras' political system has traditionally been more sensitive to the demands of peasants and labor unions and succeeded in avoiding any major internal conflict. However, the Nicaraguan scene continued to polarize internally and Honduras would gradually be pulled into the fray as a frontline country against the Sandinista regime. Only Costa Rica was spared the violence and disruption of armed rebellion.

Nicaragua became the focal point of a deepening civil unrest in the region. The FSLN openly supported the civil war in El Salvador and provided some assistance to the Guatemalan rebels. It was openly committed to promoting a political/social revolution in the region and private enterprise had little role to play in their view.

At the time of the Sandinista victory, LAAD had an outstanding exposure in Nicaragua of over $2 million divided among eleven agribusiness enterprises. Suddenly, eleven clients were reduced to only one, the Sandinista government, with whom we never were able to develop a working relationship The government soon declared a debt moratorium on its foreign obligations, mainly incurred under the administration of President Somoza, including the overseas debt of private companies expropriated by the Sandinistas. A creditor committee, consisting of Nicaragua's lead creditor banks, was formed.

As a tiny lender, LAAD played no role in these negotiations and we had little choice but to go along with the final agreements. Tom Mooney, however, did succeed in signing a separate agreement with the government on the main debt owed to LAAD, the so-called Category I debt, of about $ 1 million. The terms were very close to those negotiated by the creditor committee, but legally it was a separate contract. Tom always thought that LAAD might one day be able to work with a new Nicaraguan government, and he did not want LAAD's fortune to be entwined with the larger accord. Tom's foresight proved to be a wise move many years later.

LAAD had no choice but to cease operations in Nicaragua and to wait for a change in government and public policy. We had to write off our entire portfolio in that country over the subsequent three years. The loss of our Nicaraguan portfolio was quickly reflected in our financial statements, which, beginning in 1979, began to be hurt by significant additional loan loss reserves. In that year alone, our loss provisions rose by 70 percent to $500,000.

Abstract notions about "political risk" were suddenly transformed into specific and painful write-offs. The projects themselves did not fail, at least not initially, but they all deteriorated in the long run. We had no influence whatsoever over our borrower, the Sandinista government. We tried to protect our position, but the only practical option was to write off the entire Nicaraguan exposure and wait.

Initially, there was no secondary market for the Nicaraguan rescheduled debt, and when one did develop, the discount was so steep (over 90 percent) that we declined to sell.

Years later, when a democratic government was elected to replace the FSLN, the new government agreed to repurchase the entire foreign private debt for about ten cents on the dollar. LAAD decided not to participate in the offer, the only creditor to decline (shades of Campos Hermanos). We were able to take this position because we had signed a separate contract and were not legally bound by the master agreement.

In fact, the Sandinistas had negotiated no less than four separate rescheduling agreements, depending on the circumstances surrounding each case. LAAD participated in all four agreements and had to negotiate a solution one case at a time.

In one instance, a former borrower recovered his property from the Nicaraguan government that LAAD had previously financed. He voluntarily agreed to reinstate the principal amount of the LAAD loan as it was at the time of the expropriation and we made available to him a working capital line to help him get back in business.

Another former client received government bonds in lieu of his property and he shared them with us, thereby allowing us to make a partial recovery.

In a third case, LAAD negotiated an arrangement with the government whereby we were repaid in abandoned irrigation pipes. LAAD, in turn, sold them on a five-year payment plan to a Nicaraguan company at a price negotiated in advance with the company and the government. The Nicaraguan company then used these pipes to build irrigation systems on local farms and offered financing terms similar to those given by LAAD to the company. This was a very creative solution because it simultaneously solved the problem of the government's old debt to LAAD, put the abandoned pipe into production and helped capitalize the farms. Everybody gained.

Additional recoveries are expected. These recoveries were possible, in part because of patience and the intangible asset of having been the first foreign financial institution to resume doing business in Nicaragua following its return to democratic rule.

The political problems in Central America clearly demonstrated to us the risk of relying excessively on this market for our future growth. Although our Caribbean operations were proceeding normally, the potential for growth there was limited by the small size of the market.

Even as the Sandinistas were marching into downtown Managua, LAAD was beginning to look further south in search of new opportunities to diversify its portfolio geographically. At that time, the one country which was making the greatest progress in refocusing its priorities in favor of a free market economy was Chile under General Augusto Pinochet. That country's private sector was demonstrating an innovative spirit not seen in many decades.

We decided to explore that market and found an opportunity to help Chilean farmers take advantage of the winter fruit market in the Northern Hemisphere. This diversification proved to be so successful that Chile quickly became the largest single country in LAAD's agribusiness portfolio.

In Chile, most of our clients were well-educated professionals who had studied law, industrial engineering, accounting, economics or some other career in Chilean universities. Only a few had any background in agronomy, but they all saw the market opportunity and they put their own savings into developing it. The central valleys of Chile were well endowed to produce high quality deciduous fruit. It has a climate similar in every respect to California except for being in the counter-season.

Our clients there included Fernando Barros, who built up a parallel fruit export company, Aconex; Edmundo Miquel, who developed one small farm, then sold it and built a bigger one in association with English investors; Jose Rabat, who not only produced fruit for export, but went on to build one of the country's most successful wineries; Jorge Eyzaguirre, who rebuilt a vineyard ruined under the agrarian reform and also went on to build his own winery, which he later sold to Domaines Baron de Rothschild Lafite of France; Sergio May Colvin who transformed a barren waste land near Chacabuco north of Santiago into a productive fruit orchard; and Reid Dorn, an American, who built a table grape farm in the northern Elqui Valley famous for its early maturing grapes.

LAAD backed a number of individual fruit farmers in Curico who were among the local pioneers in developing a successful fruit export business, including Jose Alarcon, Rafael Arancibia, Victor Lozano and Patricio Marin. Thousands of Chilean businessmen risked their savings and developed that nation's now legendary winter fruit export industry.

Some of LAAD's shareholders were critical of the Chilean government's human rights record and were reluctant to vote for loans destined for that country. However, none of LAAD's funds were used to back close supporters of the government and the employment benefits in Chile's central valleys were enormous, benefits which long outlasted General Pinochet's stay in power.

Chilean entrepreneurs also made remarkable progress in developing that country's forestry resources with the help of innovative tax incentives. Chile had been a heavily forested country in the southern half of the country until the trees were cut down for raising cattle and farming. Reforestation not only created new forests, but gave new life to the country's wood and pulp industries which now export over $1 billion using a renewable resource.

These accomplishments were all the more remarkable for taking place in a country, which until recently, had considered agriculture as a social problem which could only be solved with agrarian reform and direct government intervention. The new Chilean government took the opposite tack and systematically withdrew its direct involvement and financial subsidy programs for farmers. It returned expropriated farms to those owners who had refused to sign the expropriations decree of the Allende government. Those who did sign were not given their properties back.

Government-owned enterprises in the agribusiness sector, like IANSA, the beet sugar monopoly, were systematically privatized, and forced to compete in the open market. Subsidized credit to the farming sector was eliminated. On the other hand, high tariffs on agricultural inputs were slashed along with all other tariffs, thereby making it less expensive for farmers to import farm equipment and other inputs needed to improve productivity.

LAAD's diversification into Chile was entirely financed with money borrowed from banks as AID had no meaningful program in that nation for political reasons. LAAD soon opened an office in Santiago and was planning to continue expanding in this market.

However, these plans were superseded by another 'exogenous' event out of our control. In the spring of 1982, the Mexican government declared a moratorium on paying its foreign debt, thereby precipitating the worst financial crisis in Latin America since the end of World War II. The crisis forced every country in the region to reschedule its foreign debt, except for Colombia.

For years, Latin America had been borrowing internationally because its internally generated savings were inadequate to finance its domestic investment needs. The region, and Mexico in particular, was increasingly borrowing short term to finance long term projects. This system could function only so long as the lenders remained confident of Mexico's liquidity levels and were willing to roll over old credits along with extending even larger new ones. As Mexico's international reserves dwindled, a fact the government kept carefully concealed from the outside world, the country had no alternative but to declare a moratorium.

Mexico's decision resonated throughout the region's central banks, all of whom were relying heavily on foreign borrowings to pay for their balance of trade deficits as well as internal investments. The overseas financial spigot was abruptly turned off.

Soon, Mexico's moratorium became regionalized. No one could pay. Only the international aid agencies, like the World Bank and the Interamerican Development Bank, continued to provide long term financing, but, by then, official sources of credit had been surpassed by private sources in terms of total volume. Commercial bank credit had dried up.

The magnitude of the problem had never been seen before in so many countries. It took years of painstaking negotiations, often accompanied by mutual recriminations, before governments were able to reach agreements with their creditors. Lacking the resources to finance its own growth, Latin America fell into a period of protracted economic recession, often referred to as the "lost decade."

The impact on LAAD was equally profound. Like Latin America, we went for nearly a decade without growing. We were reluctant to lend new funds, because of the difficulties in converting into hard currency payments from our existing clients and, in any event, few farmers were willing to expand during a prolonged recession. This crisis occurred while LAAD was still writing off its remaining exposure with the Nicaraguan government.

The new crisis not only threatened LAAD with substantial additional write-offs, but seriously interrupted the cash flow even from solvent borrowers, because central banks were keeping the moneys deposited with them by our clients. This development was not without its irony. Most Latin American central banks had been requiring foreign lenders to obtain prior approval for each loan. Upon approval, the loan had to be registered with the central bank. The rationale behind all this control was to assure that the purpose of the loan was in the national interest and registration was required in order to guarantee access to central bank dollars when repayment in local currency was made by the borrower. Under the terms of these registrations, our clients were required to deliver any payments in local currency for deposit with the local central bank. The central bank would then convert the local currency into dollars and remit them to our account overseas.

We had little trouble obtaining approval for the purpose of the loans, or in registering our loans. However, the registration later backfired on us. Once the debt moratoria were declared, many central banks received the local currency payments from our clients only to siphon them off in order to shore up their own weakened financial position.. Theoretically, we would have been better off making the loans through the parallel market and ignoring the central banks' guarantees, which turned out to be worthless. In practice, LAAD had no choice but to follow all central bank regulations to the letter.

LAAD had to devote endless months over a period of years of management time in patient negotiations with central bankers trying to recover its blocked funds. We used every tool we could imagine, including offering to reinvest any funds remitted to LAAD back into the country; increasing our investments in exchange for allowing the free flow of funds; reinvesting the funds locally in equity investments; accepting negotiable government bonds in exchange for the debt; and swapping debt of one country for that of another. The process of recovery took years and our strategy had to be tailor-made to the reality of each country's central bank.

In El Salvador and in Guatemala, we accepted government bonds in some cases, because both countries had a long history of meeting their foreign obligations. In Peru, we agreed to reinvest the entire proceeds from any payment received back into the country, which, in fact, we did. In Guatemala, we agreed with the country's Finance Ministry to reinvest two dollars in that country for every dollar repaid from prior loans. This arrangement applied to those loans for which we had not received government bonds, and the agreement was successful in eliminating all of the local currency then deposited with the Guatemalan Central Bank.

In Chile, we swapped part of our debt with the Chilean Central Bank for obligations of the Government of Guatemala, because we had more confidence in Guatemala than in Chile. One year later, we sold the Guatemalan bonds at a profit recovering all the loss incurred when we swapped out of Chile plus all the interest that would have accrued had we held onto that debt.

The most innovative and difficult decision was when we agreed to swap part of our outstanding Chilean debt for equity in local companies. The Central Bank authorized each transaction separately and then collected a fee for authorizing it. We used this debt to make investments in three companies: a joint venture in salmon farming, another one in scallops farming and an investment in a wholly owned sawmill and forest. In the end, we recovered almost all of the debt converted, but in the process we had to devote an enormous amount of management time, which could have been spent on more profitable endeavors.

From the Chilean debt-for-equity experience, we learned that the professional qualities needed to manage an equity portfolio are often incompatible with those needed to manage a loan portfolio. An equity investor seeks to maximize opportunities, while the lender seeks to control his risk. No one person can be good at both disciplines. In retrospect, we should perhaps have been better advised to set up a separate management team to handle the equity investments, but our holdings were too small to justify the additional cost.

In the end, LAAD recovered most of the debt held by Latin America government agencies. The main exception is Nicaragua where the company is still in the process of recovering the remaining outstanding principal, twenty years after the Sandinista victory. Patience is indeed a virtue and is sometimes rewarded.

Despite the managerial and financial disruption caused by the Latin American debt crisis, LAAD still found limited markets for its traditional project financing business. Obviously, the Latin American countries had no foreign exchange to pay for even more foreign debt. Consequently. most of LAAD's new loans during this period were used to provide pre-export financing. When structuring these loans, LAAD often negotiated an agreement with central banks whereby we could obtain payment directly from export proceeds offshore, before the funds were actually remitted to the exporter. This often took the form of retention agreements. Such arrangements cost the central banks nothing, because our money went in first and we only got paid if the money actually generated new export receipts, which served as our source of repayment.

Despite significant collection problems, LAAD never stopped doing business in Latin America even at the peak of the debt crisis. Once again, we have to thank AID for coming to our assistance at a critical time. Although LAAD was willing to take the risk and continue operating, it had no possibility whatever of raising medium term funds from the private financial community. In 1981, in the middle of the debt crisis, AID extended a third loan to LAAD in the amount of $6 million for use in Central America. AID required us to use the funds to promote non-traditional agricultural exports, which is what we were doing best and which was responsive to the challenge of the times.

The debt crisis also forced us to look at ourselves anew. By the end of 1982, it was clear that the crisis was not going away anytime soon. We were devoting much of our management time solving problems, most of which were more related to the countries' illiquidity than to our clients. Although we continued extending medium term loans, we became more active in terms of taking an equity position in new ventures. In addition to the debt conversions in Chile, LAAD also built and operated two berry farms and formed a joint venture in a berry and asparagus exporting company in Chile; a joint venture marketing company in Miami and a joint venture macadamia farm in Costa Rica. We invested in the world's only commercial conch hatchery in the Turks & Caicos Islands, Trade Wind Industries, which called for a good sense of humor.

Some of our equity investments were undertaken to recover loans lost when a client went bankrupt. This was the case of the Cool Shade ranch in Belize, the Lican forest near Entrelagos in Chile and the Sunnberry asparagus and berry farm in Angol, also in Chile. We succeeded in recovering our investment in both the forest and the ranch, but suffered a significant loss in the case of the berry farm. In all cases, the business survived and the new management has expanded production.

We looked for investment opportunities in Latin American-related businesses, but where the underlying risk was in dollars. We invested in two American technology companies, one in the sugar cane seed business, Crop Genetics International, and one a venture fund specializing in agribusiness technology, Plant Resources Venture Fund II. We even built our own office building in downtown Coral Gables.

For the first two years, the results of these investments were encouraging. Some of them were making attractive returns and the others were running ahead of expectations. These first indications turned out to be misleading.

When it became clear that we were not necessarily competent managers of businesses, we decided to go back to our basic business of project financing. We sold our office building in Coral Gables; divested our shares in Crop Genetics International, which had since gone public in the United States; shut down our Miami marketing company and sold many of our other investments back to our joint venture partners. The divestment took place over a period of several years. Sometimes we made a profit, sometimes we merely recovered our investment and sometimes we lost money. Our biggest loss occurred in our marketing subsidiary. We clearly did not know how to market imported product from Latin America into the United States.

Aside from not being competent managers of businesses, we were investing in unlisted companies, typically in countries with no established stock markets. When we wanted to sell our ownership, we faced the dilemma of how to exit the joint venture at a profit. In most instances, the only buyer was our joint venture partner, who had little incentive to pay top dollar, because he was already running the business.

We tried several formulae, most often 50-50 joint ventures. We typically included a provision in any shareholder agreement, that if either partner wanted to exit the joint venture, he would fix the value of his shares, while the other partner was given the right to buy or sell those shares at that price. On paper, this sounded fine, but if any partner failed to live up to that provision, local laws were sufficiently weak that it could not be enforced. The fact that the other partner was the managing partner, who actually ran the business, always put us in a weak negotiating position.

The Latin American debt crisis not only forced us to review our operating priorities, but also forced us to strengthen our balance sheet with better quality assets. We began purchasing long term bonds issued by international development banks, like the World Bank and the Interamerican Development Bank. At the time of purchase, these bonds were yielding rates in excess of 16 percent, a rate higher than we were charging most of our clients. As the debt crisis subsided, LAAD was able to reduce its holdings of these bonds and earn a substantial premium.

Clearly the maintenance of a high-quality bond portfolio is no substitute for good portfolio management. However, as we saw in the case of Nicaragua and the recurring foreign debt problems in Latin America, LAAD will always have to keep a portfolio of high quality marketable securities as an insurance policy against destabilizing events beyond our control.

The final lesson we learned from the Latin American debt crisis was the need to expand the number of countries where we operate. The most important reason is portfolio diversification to avoid excessive exposure in any one country.

A second reason is that monetary and fiscal policies differ among the countries, alternatively en-

Costa Rica is a leading Latin American pineapple exporter. In this picture, pineapples are being harvested by hand at Pinales de Santa Clara, S.A. in Sarapiqui, Costa Rica. LAAD has financed 193 fruit and vegetable projects totaling $84 million, making it the largest single sector in LAAD's portfolio.

LAAD has provided important financial support to the citrus industry in Belize. Orange and grapefruit juice exports have surpassed cane sugar as the country's principal industry. Henry Canton, an independent citrus farmer, stands in front of one of his orange trees near Dangriga, Belize.

Honduras has become one of Latin America's largest exporters of winter melons to the United States. A packer at the Hondex, S.A. classification plant near Choluteca, Honduras, shows a melon ready for export. Hondex is Honduras' largest grower and exporter of fresh melons.

Papayas represent a relatively new export crop from Latin America. Two plant workers employed by Papayas del Pacifico, S.A. near Golfito, Costa Rica classify and pack fresh papayas for export.

Bananas are a traditional export from Latin America and the Caribbean. New markets are being opened in Eastern Europe and mainland China. LAAD has financed new growers in Central America, while in Ecuador, Latin America's largest producer, LAAD has supported many projects designed to improve productivity and water control. The banana packing line in the picture belongs to Finca La Vega, in the state of Trujillo, Venezuala. Although primarily an oil exporter, Venezuala produces bananas on the eastern side of Lake Maracaibo.

This large irrigated tomato field is typical of the scale required to produce industrial tomatoes in a highly competitive world market. This operation is owned by Barcelo Agroindustrial in Angostura, the Dominican Republic. The growing and processing of tomatoes has become a major industry in that country. LAAD has supported other tomato growers in Anguilla, Honduras, and Peru.

One of the strongest non-traditional crops in Costa Rica is leather-leaf fern, which is exported to Western Europe and the United States. Originally developed by Florida fern growers, the leather-leaf fern does well on the slopes of the volcanoes around San Jose. This picture shows Jack Shuman, the owner of Paraiso Verde, S.A., in one of his saran-covered fern plantations near Cartago.

Probably the most dramatic transformation in recent years of one country's agriculture has taken place in Chile. That country successfully opened a winter market in the Northern Hemisphere for its deciduous fruits. This picture shows fruit trees flowerings at Sociedad Agricola La Hornilla Ltda's fruit farm in Melipilla. The company grows and ships grapes, cherries and peaches.

Primicies del Agro S.A. produces ornamental plants for export to nurseries in the United States, Europe and Japan. The project is located in San Jose Pinula, Guatemala. In the picture, a farm worker waters rows of ivy.

The macadamia nut has been introduced to Latin America. Finca Ventura in Costa Rica is one of the pioneers in the industry. LAAD entered into a 50-50 joint venture with Michael Thomas, who years earlier pioneered the cut-flower industry in Costa Rica. Finca Ventura operates its own macadamia tree nursery which is pictured here.

Floriculture has been a major part of LAAD's financing since its inception. Flower growing is the most labor intensive sector in agriculture and typically requires the largest investment per hectare. Colombia was the first Latin American country to recognize the world market potential for fresh flowers and is now the world's largest exporter of carnations. This greenhouse in the Sabana de Bogota in Colombia belongs to Tinzuke, S.A.

Neighboring Ecuador, a relative newcomer to the flower business, has established an international reputation for high quality roses that are shipped around the world. Workers at this packing house belonging to Flores Latacunga S.A. in Latacunga, Ecuador are preparing roses for export.

The cultivation of soybeans in Bolivia is transforming the Department of Santa Cruz into a growing supplier of beans, meal, and oil to world markets. Agriculture is now the fastest growing sector of the Bolivian economy. LAAD has financed many soybean projects in Bolivia, most of them experienced farmers who recently immigrated to that country from Brazil. In this picture, Ener Fluninham, who learned farming in his native Brazil, is standing in a soybean field in the Department of Santa Cruz, Bolivia.

LAAD has been less involved in financing traditional agricultural commodities, but has made a number of exceptions. This cacao farm belonging to Hummingbird Citrus Ltd. near Belmopan, Belize was financed because of its pioneering efforts to introduce this crop into Belize.

Coffee is another traditional commodity. LAAD has focused its financing on growers who produce a high quality coffee that receives a premium price on international markets. This traditional wet coffee mill owned by Finca Liquidambar, in Usumatlan, Guatemala, processes premium quality coffee at higher elevations.

LAAD has financed 81 food processing plants in the region. One of the smallest is this family owned company in Belize, Melinda Estates, which produces a range of fruit jams and hot sauces for the domestic and United States market.

couraging or discouraging project financing from abroad. At any given point of time, a few countries will offer very interesting financing opportunities, a few more will offer no opportunities and the rest are somewhere in between. As a small company, it is relatively easy for us to shift from one country to another and country diversification allows us to use that ability to our advantage.

LAAD started out as a Central American financial institution, expanded gradually into the Caribbean and then into South America. By 1982, Chile had grown to be the largest single country in LAAD's portfolio, a position it maintained for four years. It was only the difficult debt renegotiations in the mid-eighties and continued exchange controls by the central bank that forced us to reduce our Chilean exposure. We compensated for this by expanding aggressively into Bolivia and Ecuador, both of which now rank near the top of our portfolio.

Despite the debt crisis, LAAD turned in several years of record earnings, particularly in 1984 when our earnings rose to 14 per cent on net worth, our highest rate of return ever. These results were partly the result of successful problem solving, a willingness to continue operating throughout the crisis and of the purchase of high quality bonds at a time when interest rates had peaked.

Despite LAAD's willingness to continue operating during this period, the growth in the portfolio slowed noticeably from earlier years. We decided to take advantage of this slowdown by redeeming the $2.1 million in preferred participating shares that had been issued earlier to match two AID loans. Fortunately, our earnings were sufficiently strong that we could redeem the preferred shares over a three year period, continue to pay a dividend on the Common Shares and still build up our net worth in anticipation of resuming our growth in the future.

The 1980s was a period of survival and con-solidation. We solved our problems one at a time; we refocused our business around medium term project financing; and we consolidated ourselves financially by redeeming the preferred shares and building up our net worth. Once again, the stage was set for further expansion and geographic diversification.

7

A New Lease on Life

The Latin American debt crisis slowly began to resolve itself one country at a time. Solutions were tailor-made for each country and its creditors. Some involved debt-for-equity swaps; others partial forgiveness, still others buyouts at a steep discount, but most called for restructuring and rescheduling, a la Brady plan. First, a restructuring agreement would be signed by a country with its respective creditor committee, then the new notes would be securitized and then the secondary market would set a value on the new notes. Lenders who wanted to leave the region could do so at the market discount, while other more risk tolerant investors would buy the notes for their high yield. That allowed investors to begin looking for new opportunities in Latin America instead of merely cleaning up yesterday's mess.

The solution of the debt crisis coincided with the biggest realignment in macro-economic policies in Latin America since the end of World War II. One country after another followed Chile's lead in the 1970s by opening up their economies to international competition; import tariffs were slashed; foreign exchange controls dismantled; budget deficits were reduced and often eliminated; state-owned corporations were privatized; and foreign investment encouraged. In some ways, the prolonged recession may have encouraged politicians to accelerate the process, because it was patently clear that the old policies underwritten by the Alliance For Progress were not working. New ideas were needed, even when they dated back several hundred years. They were heady days, and the process is still on-going.

LAAD was anxious to take advantage of these new market opportunities, but Latin America's financial reputation was so damaged that LAAD still remained unattractive to the international financial markets. We again made the rounds of the international lending agencies and we were again turned down for a variety of reasons.

For the sixth and, mercifully, last time, we turned again to AID for support. In 1986, AID responded with a $15 million (later increased to $20 million) for use in Central America. Both the timing and the amount of the loan were critical to LAAD's ability to grow its business again on a self-sustaining basis.

Once again, world realpolitik worked in our favor. Although the Soviet Union had embraced *glasnost'* and *perestroika* under Mikhail Gorbachev, the Sandinistas remained active in their efforts to destabilize Central America and Fidel Castro could always be counted on to make a fiery speech denouncing the United States. Consequently, the American foreign aid program in Latin America was still receiving strong congressional support and the idea of supporting the private sector was particularly timely.

AID was satisfied that LAAD's capital base and financial performance were sufficiently strong that they did not require us to increase our capital base. Rather, we were asked to provide an additional $3 million to the joint program, but it was up to us whether to raise our capital or to borrow the funds. We chose to borrow.

For the first time in its history, LAAD was in a strong position to grow. The debt crisis of the 1980s discouraged us from growing and encouraged us to reinvest our earnings and build a strong capital base. We had no difficulty taking on the latest AID loan and even had additional resources available for investment outside of Central America.

By 1990, we had made our first loan to Venezuela for a mango farm, Agro Austral, designed to sell in the European market. In 1991, we opened three new offices in David, Panama; San Pedro Sula, Honduras; and Santa Cruz de la Sierra, Bolivia. In that same year, we made our first loan to Ecuador to a flower farm in the mountains near the town of Latacunga.

We expanded our modest investments in Peru and we returned to Nicaragua in 1992 with Violeta Chamorro's electoral victory and the return of democratic rule after a fourteen-year absence.

Our first priority, though, was clearly to place the newly signed loan from AID for Central America.

LAAD first turned to some of its traditional clients such as Michael Thomas in Costa Rica and Arturo Don Melo in Panama. These dynamic entrepreneurs were still creating new businesses and needed our medium term lending capability. In addition, new agroindustries were being developed in the region.

Costa Rica's democratic society continued to attract individual American investors. The ornamental plant industry, including leatherleaf fern and tropical plants, offered attractive investment opportunities for people with the necessary experience and a number of American individuals moved to that country. LAAD worked with many of them, including Rodney Griffith, Kenneth Lanier, John Marsell, Jack Shuman, Ken and Kitty Smith.

Guatemala took note of Costa Rica's success in this industry and followed suit with similar projects taking advantage of Guatemala's favorable climate. In addition, coffee growers were looking for profitable alternatives to their traditional crop which was passing through a period of low prices. This led to the rapid development of the cardamom and sesame seed industries, both of which received substantial financial support from LAAD.

Honduras found a niche for itself in the winter melon market, becoming the dominant Central American producer in the process. Businessmen in that country identified a variety of new export products, including frozen yucca, "tostones" (fried plantain chips) for the New York City school system, shrimp farming along the Gulf of Fonseca, baby vegetables, pineapple, citrus, and processed wood products, such as broom handles and furniture parts.

In the case of Nicaragua, LAAD had to wait several years until the return of democratic rule, before it could use AID funds in that country. We were the first foreign financial institution to resume doing business in that country, a testimony to the good experience we had with our clients prior to the Sandinista takeover. Our first new loan in that country was made to Industrias Amerrisque, a slaughterhouse in the town of Juliapa, which had been recently returned to its original owners, the Arguello family. Nicaragua is the only Central American country with the potential to become a beef exporting country. The reprivatized company lacked working capital to purchase sufficient cattle to operate the plant efficiently and turned to LAAD for financing. Within weeks of the disbursement, a number of disgruntled Sandinistas, members of the old politicized union, took temporary control of the plant, stole meat inventory and generally disrupted efforts to get the plant running again. Although their efforts eventually failed, it was a warning to us to proceed carefully as we reentered that still politicized market.

We soon found a new area of opportunity, the peanut industry. Nicaragua has ample land along the Pacific coast for agriculture. Prior to the Sandinistas, that area had been planted mainly in cotton, but the cotton growers fled the country when the Sandinistas took power and the industry soon disintegrated. Several leading Nicaraguan agribusiness firms, like Industrias Nacionales Agricolas, Maniceros de Nicaragua and Servicio Agricola Gurdian, decided that peanuts offered an attractive alternative to cotton, given the low production costs in Nicaragua compared to such major producers as Argentina and the United States. All three companies, along with their shareholders, went into the business of growing peanuts, and purchased three processing plants to shuck and classify peanuts for export. LAAD financed all three plants.

Once the placement of the final AID loan was well underway, we started looking elsewhere for expansion opportunities that would provide for long term growth. We soon focused our attention on three Andean nations, Bolivia, Ecuador and Peru. At the time we made this decision, the three countries were in various stages of reforming their economies, with Bolivia being the furthest along.

Our initial efforts in Bolivia were slowed as we tried to negotiate a local source of long term funding in indexed bolivianos. We eventually lined up the equivalent of $3 million in long term funds from FUNDAPRO, a Bolivian nonprofit foundation with close ties to the local AID mission.

This country, with its long tradition as a mineral exporting nation, was beginning to show interest in its agricultural potential. We had difficulty, though, identifying Bolivians willing to invest in farming. That country's agrarian reform had ruined the country's commercial farmers and replaced them with small Indian families living on the border of subsistence. We soon found a growing class of immigrant farmers originally from Brazil and Japan, as well as some Mennonite farmers who had immigrated from Mexico.

Very few of LAAD's farmer clients in Bolivia have Spanish sounding surnames. Most of them are Brazilians from Mato Grosso, Parana, Santa Catarina, and Rio Grande do Sul , such as Carlos Andia Veizaga, Roberto Borg, Paulo Borgo, Arli Cesconetto, Cezar Buznello, Neuri Dalmina,

Nicolau Flumingham, Arno Netzlaff and Arlindo Pontremolez, among others. They were all farmers in their native Brazil who sold their land and purchased fertile undeveloped land in Bolivia's Department of Santa Cruz. These are modern-day pioneers, who suffer the rigors and hardships of all innovators. They all grow soybeans, which they rotate with such other crops as sorghum, wheat, sunflower seed, corn, and, occasionally, cotton.

Typical of them is Mr. Arno Netzlaff and his son, Rainer. They moved to Bolivia two years before LAAD funded their 6,800 hectare farm, known as Tacuari. Mr. Netzlaff was born into a farming family in Brazil's state of Rio Grande do Sul. Land became very expensive there, so the family moved to Mato Grosso where they grew soybeans and corn, and raised cattle. Mr. Netzlaff was one of the first Brazilians to scout out the possibility of farming in Bolivia, where he bought a farm in 1992, at which point he sold off all his assets in Brazil and moved his family to Santa Cruz. Within one year they had increased their farm's area under cultivation from the 300 hectares to 1,500 hectares. In keeping with government environmental rules, they have kept a 60 meter stretch of forest every 200 meters to protect the environment. They have already experimented with no-till cultivation, which they plan to adopt once the land has become flat enough.

Japanese immigrants from Okinawa following the end of World War II established two well-organized colonies in Bolivia's Department of Santa Cruz. LAAD financed three farmers from the Yapacani colony; Sumuto Fujita, Susumu Ogata and Hikari Yonekura. In addition to soybeans, they grow rice and raise poultry for the local market.

Individually, these Brazilian pioneers and their families spend most of their waking hours building their farms and homes. Collectively, they are changing the Bolivian economy. Bolivia has traditionally been a mineral dominated economy with tin and gold, plus the more recent addition of natural gas. Today, however, the fastest growing sector in the Bolivian economy is agriculture, and the most dynamic crop is the soybean, which is sold on international markets.

Although our main focus in Bolivia has been supporting the family farmer, LAAD also financed one soybean crushing and oil extraction plant. The Industrias de Aceite plant is located in Warmes not far from Santa Cruz and is owned by the Romero group of Peru. This plant sells refined cooking oil on the local market and also ships part of its production to southern Peru. The Brazilian immigrant farmers in Bolivia are its predominant source of soybean production.

In Peru itself, LAAD quickly identified the asparagus industry as the agribusiness with the greatest growth potential. We financed a total of five projects in this industry, including growing, packing for export, canning, freezing and preserving in glass jars. Production extends along the coastal region from the southern Ica Valley to the northern plains around Piura. In Peru, asparagus farmers have adapted to desert conditions and use water to bring on hibernation rather than relying on winter weather, which is the case in temperate climates. By using this method, Peruvian farmers have more control over harvesting dates, which lets them target special windows of opportunity when world prices tend to be higher.

One of the pioneers in this industry has been Fruticola Agricola del Sur owned and managed by Jorge Checa and his son. They are credited with starting the fresh asparagus export industry from the Ica Valley in collaboration with American produce marketing companies. They have succeeded in establishing an international reputation for high-quality asparagus, which has helped make Peru the world's second-largest exporter of asparagus products. LAAD financed both the growing of asparagus as well as the construction of an asparagus canning factory in Ica.

The Checa family is also credited with being Peru's first grower and exporter of table grapes and Black Mission figs for the fresh market. The table grapes are harvested in time to make market prior to the Christmas season when prices are higher. LAAD financed both projects.

LAAD also supported the mango industry in northern Peru around the cities of Piura and Sullana. Again, Peru is fortunate in that its harvest comes during the first two months of the year, when world prices are at the their peak. In addition to financing five mango producers, LAAD also supported the construction of a hot water treatment plant, a process necessary for the fruit to meet fitosanitary requirements in the United States.

Although Peru's desert offers unique opportunities, it is located close to the Pacific Ocean and is vulnerable to heavy unseasonal rains caused by the El Nino. Peru's agriculture was particularly devastated by flooding rivers, heavy rains and soil erosion during the 1997-98 El Nino weather phenomenon. These storms caused considerable damage to LAAD's clients in that country as well as in other Pacific coast nations. In each case, we had to reschedule loans and often extend additional financing to allow our client to recover from the disaster. Changing weather patterns are part of the high risk associated with agriculture. For LAAD, it has proven much easier to deal with weather-related phenomena than with political upheavals like the Sandinistas or the bad financial management associated with the debt crisis of the 1980s.

In Ecuador, LAAD emphasized the growing of flowers (primarily roses and gypsophila) in the highlands and bananas along the coastal plains. The flower industry has become a major business in Ecuador only in the last decade. Its primary attraction is the uniform number of light hours during the day and the luminosity, all of which favor the production of high quality roses with an unusually long shelf life. This is an important competitive advantage considering the long distances the flowers must travel before making market. Ecuadoran roses are gaining market share from Colombia in both the U.S. and West European markets, and they are beginning to enter nontraditional markets. For example, thanks to the long shelf life of Ecuadoran roses, they are shipped as far away as the flower markets in Kazakhstan. To get there, the roses are first flown from Quito to the flower auction in Amsterdam and from there they are trucked all the way across Europe and the Russian steppes to Central Asia. Flowers are now Ecuador's second-largest agricultural export after bananas.

LAAD has financed a total of seven flower growers, most of them producing roses. One of these flower companies is Flores de la Montana, a rose farm near Cayanbe, owned jointly by Mr. Andres Cardenas Monge of Ecuador and the company's founder; Mr. Arturo Harker, a flower grower from Colombia; and Mr. Alvaro Varela, a Colombian living in Miami responsible for marketing the company's flowers in the United States. Colombian flower growers are becoming increasingly involved in developing production in Ecuador because of the better light conditions, and the abundance of water. This labor intensive company generates several hundred full-time jobs and exports over $3 million a year.

Also in Ecuador, LAAD worked closely with one of its shareholders, the Dole Food Company, which is the country's largest banana exporter. Dole buys its bananas from Ecuadoran farmers who receive technical assistance and advice from Dole. LAAD has financed fourteen banana growers, primarily to allow them to improve water control through better irrigation and drainage. This investment proved to be timely in 1997, when many banana growing regions were flooded by heavy rains associated with El Nino. Those growers who had invested in proper drainage suffered significantly less damage than their less provident neighbors.

More recently, we decided to enter the Venezuelan market. We had previously regarded this country as one with few opportunities in agriculture, because the economy is so dominated by oil and other mineral resources. Upon closer look, we found that the country is internationally competitive in gourmet coffee, high quality cacao, bananas, plantains, and shrimp farming.

Venezuela is one of the world's largest producers of plantains with 50,000 hectares planted around El Vigia to the southeast of Lake Maracaibo. LAAD financed Agropecuaria La Providencia, a company founded by Roberto Weill and his wife Isela, and presently managed by their three sons, Rolando, Roberto, and Rafael. The Weill family originally came from Cuba which it fled after the Communist takeover. Their business is completely integrated with their own plantain plantations, their own packinghouse, a company that offers technical assistance to other plantain growers, a factory processing fried plantain and yucca chips for the snack market, and a marketing company in Miami. The group buys most of its plantains from independent growers and ships fresh plantains to the Hispanic market in the United States as well as to Latin America and the Caribbean. They are Venezuela's largest exporters of fresh plantains.

LAAD was finally growing again in Central America, the Caribbean and in the Andean countries. All of this growth had to be financed and we needed to identify new private sources of capital. AID had already contributed more than its share by supporting us during our early and most difficult years. It was clear from previous efforts, that we could not count on financial support from any of the other international development agencies.

In 1992, we made two major breakthroughs in finding new borrowing sources. First, we drew down $2.5 million in medium term funds from CBI General Partners, Inc., a partnership of large, mostly U.S., corporations operating in Puerto Rico

under Section 936 of the U.S. tax code. This provision provided tax benefits to corporations manufacturing in Puerto Rico provided they reinvested
their earnings in eligible activities, which included
loans to small businesses in certain Caribbean Ba-
sin countries. Many of LAAD's projects qualified
under this law. Over the coming six years, we
drew down a total of $13 million from this source,
and became its largest single borrower.

Secondly, we were able to place a bond issue in
Panama for use in that country. At the time, the
Panamanian government was trying to encourage
lending to agriculture by providing tax-free treatment to private investors willing to channel their
funds into agriculture. We were qualified for the
tax exemption as a lender to Panamanian agriculture. The Panamanian branch of the Banque
Nationale de Paris then underwrote a $5 million
five-year bond issue, which was mostly subscribed
by local commercial banks and insurance companies. The bond issue was quoted on the Panamanian Stock Exchange and became the first issue
qualifying as an international bond on that exchange.

One year later, we built on that success by raising another $5 million in medium term notes un-
derwritten by the Miami Agency of Britain's
Barclays Bank. Unlike the first bond issue which
was limited to Panama, this new issue could be
used throughout Latin America. By the end of
1998, the Barclays Bank had syndicated three medium loan issues totaling $40 million. All of the
subscribers to these notes were commercial banks,
including Banco Mercantil of Venezuela and its
American subsidiary Commercebank; Banco

Espirito Santo of Portugal; Hamilton Bank, Pacific National Bank and Republic National Bank, all of Miami, and the Colonial Bank of Alabama.

In addition, we were able to raise significant amounts of money medium term directly from individual commercial banks. Until the late 1980s, LAAD had to rely primarily on short term revolving lines (180 days or less) from commercial banks. As the Latin American debt crisis receded, LAAD began asking its bankers to extend longer maturities on its borrowings. It would normally take several years before we could even raise the tenor from 180 days to two years, and several more before we could persuade a bank to provide five-year funding. Again, patience paid off.

Our earliest success was with European banks, which generally take a longer term view of their loans to Latin America than their American counterparts. They include, in addition to Barclays Bank, Dresdner Bank Lateinamerika which alone has already lent us $15 million, Banco Exterior de Espana and one shareholder bank, the Rabobank Nederland, which has provided $11 million in medium term funding in addition to interest rate swap facilities.

It was not until 1998, that we were finally able to obtain funding from an American bank, the Bank of Boston, on a medium term basis. LAAD has now raised over $70 million in medium-term funding since it began to tap the international capital market, 40 percent more than AID lent us during our first twenty years.

Our efforts to raise commercial bank funding were initially hindered at every turn by the regulatory agencies and central banks of the home country of our lending banks. These regulatory agencies routinely classified Latin American risk by country of incorporation and imposed mandatory reserve requirements for all loans made by the commercial banks under their jurisdiction to all clients in the borrowing country. It mattered not what the financial condition or the managerial competence of the borrower was; it only mattered which country the borrower was located in.

LAAD is incorporated in Panama, and Panama was classified as a high-risk country for many years until well after its public sector debt was restructured. Consequently, LAAD was classified as a Panamanian risk, even though only a small percentage of its assets were ever located in that country.

In some cases, our lending banks eventually persuaded their regulatory agencies that LAAD was a U.S. risk, because our shareholders are mostly American, our accounts are kept in dollars; our administrative office is located in Florida, we are audited according to generally accepted accounting principles in the United States; all of our loans are dollar denominated; and because we maintain a significant portfolio of dollar denominated internationally marketable bonds. LAAD could reasonably be classified as a Latin American regional risk, but no regulatory agency has a provision for regional companies.

In the case of some of our lenders, we were forced to pay back loans and end a banking relationship that stretched back many years because of these regulations. That was the case with the Bank of Tokyo, which was never able to convince the Bank of Japan that LAAD was not a Panamanian risk. The Bank of Tokyo had to cancel its credit lines with LAAD.

For years LAAD worked hard to build a financial track record of strong earnings, high liquidity ratios, a low debt/equity ratio and a strong cash flow from collections. Management turnover at the company was low and lenders gradually gained confidence about the long-term continuity of its financial performance.

Most importantly, we had to prove that we could keep the quality of our agribusiness portfolio at an acceptable level. We faced a never-ending struggle to support high-risk private agricultural enterprises without sacrificing loan quality. LAAD's nonperforming loans stand at under 4 percent of its agribusiness portfolio, while the annual write-off of these loans has averaged less than seven tenths of one percent of the portfolio since the company was founded.

Today, LAAD routinely accesses the international capital market to match its lending demand. Rates and tenor are determined by the market place and its assessment of our financial strength and debt servicing capacity.

LAAD has demonstrated to its shareholders and to the financial markets that it is capable of putting private funds paying market interest rates into agribusiness projects in Latin America and provide a reasonable rate of return to its shareholders. It has been paying back its subsidized funding from AID for over twenty years to the point that AID represents less than 15 percent of total resources, without affecting the company's profitability.

At the same time, LAAD never changed its mission of encouraging private enterprise in agriculture even after we stopped receiving subsidized funding from AID. We showed that it was profitable to finance risky developmental activities in Latin America using funds raised from the international capital markets. Most importantly, we proved that the original vision of the founding shareholders was a sound one.

LAAD's mission was possible.

8

The Bottom Line: Development

When our shareholders' treasurers made their equity contribution to LAAD in 1970, they did so in the belief that their new venture would make a difference in supporting Latin American agriculture. There must have been much good faith and optimism with such a modest capital base. The challenge to LAAD's management was how to take $2.4 million in seed capital and make it grow productively.

LAAD could clearly not be all things to all people. We had to concentrate our efforts on what we considered to be the top priority issues. Some of our friends, including AID, would have been delighted to see us involve ourselves directly with the very poor, much the way micro lending companies do today. Under this approach, we could lend a few hundred dollars to each client to purchase basic agricultural tools. We could provide working capital to small farmers to cover their annual needs prior to harvest. Some private groups have recently succeeded in creating a viable business around this concept, but back in 1970, neither LAAD's founders nor its management thought this was a practical alternative.

Development means different things to different people. To most economists, development means a sustained growth in per capita income. This measurement is the one which most accurately differentiates living standards among countries.

To the political left, notions of equality may better define their concept. Thus, a reduction in the income gap between the rich and the poor; or the difference between the earnings of an average employee and the return on invested capital, may more accurately reflect this approach. Social progress, such as improved educational opportunities, better health, or a longer life span for the average citizen, are also commonly used to measure general well being. We could even look at home and car ownership, the number of telephones per capita or the average caloric intake per day. The potential list goes on and on.

Without reviving this debate here, LAAD decided that, for Latin America, the two most important economic benefits that the company could realistically impact are rural jobs and foreign exchange earnings. Without claiming any theoretical advantage to our choices, they continue to make common sense today thirty years later.

With its initial $2.4 million paid-in capital, LAAD has since cumulatively invested over $300 million in 700 agribusiness projects in twenty-four countries throughout much of Latin America and the Caribbean. These projects are estimated to have generated at least 50,000 new full time jobs and $500-600 million in new annual export earnings. Those numbers summarize the economic impact of almost thirty years development work, one project at a time.

The first of these, jobs, is a long-term goal, one unlikely to change regardless of the relative level of development. Jobs are just as contentious a political issue in the United States today as they are in Latin America. Every citizen should have the ability and right to earn his livelihood. In LAAD's case, we refined it slightly by giving priority to rural jobs in recognition of our shareholders' commitment to agribusiness. The lower productivity prevailing in Latin American agriculture has forced millions of marginal farmers to migrate from the countryside to urban centers unable to absorb them. This massive migration has created major social problems as cities try to cope with the new arrivals who typically have few skills to offer in a highly competitive labor market. Large-scale unemployment has been a permanent feature of the Latin American landscape since the end of World War II and it shows few signs of abating.

LAAD has made a conscious effort to support projects which provide employment opportunities in rural areas. In fairness to our clients, we should restate the fact that it is they who, in fact, create the jobs. LAAD's role is to provide them with the financial resources to expand.

As a rule, we found that projects generating the highest number of jobs coincide with crops which create the highest value added per hectare. In agriculture today, the highest value added comes from intensive farming typically associated with floriculture and horticulture. A hectare of land in Costa Rica producing leatherleaf fern generates about $30,000 per year in farm gate sales, whereas one hectare in neighboring Nicaragua used for cattle raising would produce barely $700 annually. One hectare of leatherleaf fern, even when fully automated, will require about six full time workers in the field and the packing house, whereas it would take about four hectares of pasture for cattle to employ one person full time. The labor intensity per hectare of leatherleaf fern is over twenty times that of cattle raising.

The comparison is even more striking in the case of growing roses. In the highlands around Quito, a rose farmer will generate about $350,000 in farm gate sales or 500 (!) times more than cattle ranching. Employment on a rose farm comes to about thirty-five workers per hectare or 140 times more jobs than the cattle ranch. Obviously, the capital investment per hectare in the case of the roses is substantially higher than in the cattle industry. The point here is that land has the capacity to support many more jobs, and higher paying ones, than in traditional activities such as cattle grazing.

Job opportunities may also be created indirectly in other sectors. For many decades, the major economic activity on the island of Chiloe in southern Chile was growing potatoes, mostly by small farmers who barely sustained their families. Poorly educated and with few local employment opportunities, they were typical candidates to migrate to Santiago. This activity generated few jobs, except for the small farmers themselves and their families. Today, the island is a world leader in raising Atlantic salmon for international markets. The job market has grown dramatically, with demand for marine biologists and skilled labor both for raising and packing the salmon. Potato farming has become an incidental industry, much like vegetable gardening in suburbia. Furthermore, the salmon industry is integrated with fresh water hatcheries, trucking, feed mills, packing and freezing plants, all of which generate substantial additional good paying jobs.

Many of LAAD's projects have significant impacts in the local economy surrounding area. The company once took over a Chilean raspberry farm, because it had become insolvent. The farm had about sixty hectares of good farm land near the southern town of Angol. Unable to find a buyer for the farm, LAAD set out to rehabilitate it prior to selling it, just as the company had done with the Cool Shade ranch in Belize. The company micro-leveled the land and built an irrigation system using water from a nearby canal. We planted the farm in different varieties of raspberries, blackberries, red currants, blueberries, persimmon, and asparagus. These high-value crops produce in the neighborhood of $20,000 in export sales per hectare. This particular crop mix allowed the farm to start harvesting operations in September with the asparagus and continue all through the summer season until the persimmon were harvested in the early fall. The farm employed forty full-time workers and hired up to 350 field hands during the long harvest period. Although not large in area, the farm was the largest single employer in the Angol area.

Neighbors began planting the same crops and a freezing plant was built across the street. The whole crop pattern in the neighboring farms was changed. The town soon acquired the trappings of prosperity like repaving its streets, planting flowers in the parks, building new housing and a tennis club. The town, which used to provide maids to Santiago, is now able to provide employment opportunities locally. Angol has gone through a remarkable transformation.

These examples demonstrate the potential of modern agribusiness to bring dynamic job opportunities to rural areas and to integrate them into the national and international economies.

About two thirds of LAAD's disbursements to date have gone to business activities that generate high rural employment. Over 50 percent of LAAD's portfolio consists of floriculture and horticulture projects alone.

Not everyone agrees that job creation should top the list of development priorities. Several years after LAAD started operating, we received a letter from a religious organization in New York City, with a copy sent to the chairmen of all of our shareholders for maximum effect. The letter complained that 7 percent of LAAD's portfolio was devoted to flower farms, whose production was destined for middle-class American households. The implication was that we were benefiting middle-class Americans rather than producing more food for the poor and hungry in Latin America.

In response to this letter, I flew to Colombia to visit our most recent flower project, involving a $200,000 loan disbursed in 1973 to a recently established company, AGRODEX. This company had been created by German Torres Lozano, a Colombian, and Daniel Gelfman, an American. Mr. Lozano managed the production side in Colombia while Mr. Gelfman organized a new marketing company in Miami. Neither had any prior experience in flower growing, but they recognized a growth opportunity and invested their own savings in their new venture. They had purchased a sixteen-hectare piece of land in the Sabana de Bogota and had already built their first greenhouse. LAAD's loan was intended to allow them to expand and to provide needed working capital. The flowers were initially intended for the United States market where middle-class America did indeed represent a major undertapped market.

Greenhouses were being built on 2.5 hectares of their land. We compared what the land use had been before and after the flower farm was built. The results were striking. That land had originally been used for dairy farming with an occasional potato crop on part of the land, employing the equivalent of half a person on a full time basis on the 2.5 hectares in question. The new flower farm required sixty full-time workers and professionals with full social and medical benefits. The employment ratio between the old and the new land use was over 120:1 in favor of the greenhouse. Today, that same borrower employs a full-time work force of 2,200 people, a remarkable example of what an innovative, private enterprise can create out of a market opportunity.

The answer to the criticism of funding flowers vs. food was that people who earn a decent wage do not go hungry; they buy their food on the open market. There has rarely been a food shortage in any Latin American economy with an open market system; but rather a lack of purchasing power by poor people to buy food. Job creation gives employees that purchasing power.

We have tried to measure the jobs created by the projects we finance. Although there is an inevitable level of arbitrariness in any measuring system, we decided to take the expected employment once the project had reached its capacity as a result of LAAD's financing. On average, we found that it took about $7,500 of LAAD's money to create one full-time job equivalent. Most of these jobs were full time, but a number were also seasonal jobs calculated on a full-time equivalency. Crop cycles dictate employment patterns in agriculture. Modern agriculture sometimes makes it possible to extend the natural crop cycle, and therefore employment, through irrigation, drainage, crop management, mix of crops and the use of greenhouses.

Some people, particularly in the United States, complain that these new industries, such as flowers in Colombia, ferns in Costa Rica and asparagus in Peru, were created to exploit low prevailing wages. We have not found this to be the case. What attracts new investment to agriculture in Latin America is favorable weather conditions, the opportunity to produce crops destined for specific market windows, and the logistics of shipping perishable products to market economically with sufficient shelf life.

The volcanoes around San Jose, Costa Rica provide ideal climatic and soil conditions to grow leatherleaf fern; the same is true for carnations in the plains around Bogota, Colombia; roses around Quito, Ecuador, asparagus along the coastal desert of Peru; deciduous fruits in the central valleys of Chile, and raising salmon in the cold fjords of southern Chile. If wages had been the motivating factor, all of these activities would have located in

Haiti. We know of no agricultural activity in Latin America, with the possible exception of the northern Mexican border with the United States, where wages play a significant role in locating a business.

LAAD's second development priority is the generation of foreign exchange earnings. This goal may prove more ephemeral than job creation, but will probably remain a priority for a number of years more. The level of savings in Latin America remains inadequate to sustain the region's investment needs. To fill that gap, Latin America must borrow abroad or attract foreign investment. If Latin America is to service these foreign obligations, it will have to increase its export earnings. The relative impact of this goal will inevitably decline as Latin America becomes more developed.

Historically, virtually all of the world's developed economies graduated from prolonged stagnation to growth through new export industries. These industries allowed countries to specialize in what they do best and to break out of the constraints imposed by a limited local market. Agricultural commodities often led the way, such as the English woolen textiles and Portuguese port used by classical economists to demonstrate the advantages of free trade.

Every single Latin American country experienced sustained growth in per capita income, often going back into the nineteenth century. Virtually all of it was fueled by the export of basic commodities to world markets.

Brazil began to grow by exporting sugar and then coffee to world markets. During the last century, Chile began shipping wheat to gold-crazed

Californians until the construction of the transcontinental railroad. Ecuador shipped cacao. Belize and Cuba both exported cane sugar, although on a totally different scale. Argentina was built on wool, meat, and wheat. Guatemala, Costa Rica, and Colombia produced the better-quality coffee at higher elevations. Large investments in other basic commodities like minerals and oil played a similar role in the early development of the Latin American economies. Together, they provided the demand for further domestically oriented investments in public utilities, like railroads, power, and telephones.

The end of World War II brought an initial boom in agricultural exports from Latin America as the region took advantage of the damage caused to productive capacity in other parts of the world However, as the rest of the world recovered, commodity prices declined and Latin America was left wondering what to do next.

It was at this point that a new generation of Latin American economists, such as Raul Prebisch, proposed reducing the region's dependence on commodity exports and restructuring the local economies as we discussed earlier.

A central economic theme of these arguments was concern over the shortage of foreign exchange. In order to develop, everyone knew that Latin America would require foreign exchange to purchase the capital equipment needed to modernize and to develop new industries. If commodity exports were incapable of accomplishing this, then they had to look elsewhere, and they chose import substitution.

Most Latin American economies in the postwar years grew through substituting imported industrial products. Unfortunately, very few of these new industries were capable of competing internationally, and they could only survive behind high external tariffs. These inefficient industries along with years of government budget deficits led to years of hyperinflation and financial chaos in the domestic markets. Profitability was determined not by improving efficiency and increasing production capacity but by astute cash management. This strategy of import substitution proved to be unsustainable.

As we mentioned earlier, Chile was the first Latin American country to break away from the import substitution model and to open the economy up to international competition. The effect of this decision was swift and dramatic. Investors quickly shifted their focus and money away from the once favored import substitution industries in favor of new exporting activities. Chile had clear competitive advantages in agriculture, fishing, forestry, and mining and they were the sectors which led Chile to where it is today. The generation of foreign exchange earnings through exports was the key. The results of this strategy were not lost on Chile's neighbors who gradually introduced similar policies with similar results.

Once dependent on the largesse of sympathetic politicians, Latin American agriculture has become a growth sector thanks to the new international marketing opportunities made possible by falling tariffs in the world's major markets.

LAAD recognized these opportunities and decided to emphasize nontraditional agricultural exports almost from the outset. This decision represented a convergence of our developmental policy of generating new foreign exchange earnings and a recognition of the growing markets for nontraditional crops around the world. Luckily for LAAD and its clients, the world's leading trading nations had committed themselves to promoting freer world trade and were determined to lower trade barriers.

Focusing on foreign exchange earnings benefited LAAD in several operational ways. Most importantly, companies which generate foreign exchange through exports typically are better able to repay hard currency debts than those which sell domestically for local currency. The main reason is the risk of losses caused by exchange rate fluctuations.

Latin America went through many years of high inflation, which was always accompanied by frequent and violent devaluations of the local currency against the dollar. Although inflation and devaluation move in the same direction, they rarely move at the same rate or timing. Short-term disparities in the rates of inflation and devaluation create major exchange risks to companies borrowing in one currency and selling in another. The financial cost of borrowed funds create windfall gains when local interest rates fall below the rate of inflation or devaluation, but they can cause a cost squeeze when the foreign exchange rate against the dollar is frozen as a means of controlling inflation. In this case, local costs will climb with inflation, while the local currency equivalent of exports is frozen. Companies can go bankrupt for reasons unrelated to their basic business, but rather to the way their business is financed. All of

LAAD's loans are denominated in dollars so its clients' exposure to foreign exchange related losses are substantially reduced when its clients sell in hard currency markets.

A classic example of massive bankruptcies caused by foreign exchange risk occurred in Chile toward the end of the 1970s, when the Central Bank decided to hold the exchange rate fixed at thirty-nine pesos to the dollar in order to keep inflation under control and to encourage stable financial markets. Its anti-inflationary policy also included restrictions on expansion in the money supply which caused local currency interest rates to soar. They exceeded 40 percent annually for over a year. In the absence of any devaluation, this meant that the borrowers were paying 40 percent in hard currency terms. No legal business can afford to pay 40 percent interest in hard currency for very long. Consequently, the country's fruit producers, although enjoying favorable overseas markets for their goods, fell in arrears on a massive scale, followed soon by bankruptcies. When banks foreclosed on the mortgaged farms, they found that the market value of farm land had collapsed, and the banks were unable to recover their principle through foreclosure. The banks themselves were then threatened with bankruptcy, which was only forestalled by massive Central Bank intervention. Eventually, the country had to devalue the peso; default on its foreign debt; financial markets were thrown into a turmoil; and the country had to go through another bout of high inflation. Central bankers are sometimes their own worst enemies.

What was the impact of LAAD's operations on Latin America's hard currency earnings? Again,

the numbers are somewhat arbitrary. We used export earnings expected when the project reaches a
stable production level.

Statistically speaking, the greatest impact is generated by processing plants, such as slaughterhouses, freezing or canning plants and packing
plants. These plants often generate foreign exchange
earnings many times higher than the required investment. That is because they process locally purchased
raw materials and transform them into a product
in demand internationally.

Farm projects producing the raw materials, on
the other hand, appear to show a lower impact.
The contrasting impact is more apparent than real.
All agribusiness systems must work in tandem and
it can be quite arbitrary trying to assign a higher
impact to any segment of an integrated system.

Over the years, we found that one dollar dis-
bursed by LAAD eventually will generate close to
two dollars of annual export earnings, although
the numbers vary significantly from one industry
to another. In the case of the Colombian flower
farm mentioned earlier, the 2.5 hectares initially
produced $250,000 in export earnings at the farm
gate. Today, that same company ships $14 million
and is one of the top three flower exporting companies in Colombia.

Overall, we estimate that LAAD financing allows our clients to generate $500-600 million in
additional hard currency earnings per year. These
numbers represent a tiny fraction of the more than
$200 billion in annual exports from Latin America
and the Caribbean, but it looks more respectable
when measured against the $2.4 million seed
money originally invested in LAAD.

Although job creation and the generation of hard currency exports remain today our top two developmental priorities, LAAD does look at other issues. One of AID's objectives in supporting LAAD was to provide better opportunities to small farmers and poor people in rural areas. Projects meeting these goals were typically food processing plants, which bought raw materials from small farmers and employed large numbers of workers, often women, in classifying and packaging the final product.

The most efficient way of reaching poor farmers is through an intermediary which will purchase their production. We have found that a processing plant purchasing high-value annual crops, such as vegetables is an effective way of putting capital in the hands of small farmers. In this case, the processing plant would typically sign a contract with the farmers to purchase their crop at a minimum price, advance inputs (using our money) such as seed, fertilizers, and agricultural chemicals, and provide technical assistance on how to use the inputs. The important point here is not that resources were channeled into the hands of poor farmers, but that the farmers became more productive as a result of the financing and their incomes rose in proportion to their productivity.

Another area of secondary interest to LAAD has been the encouragement of new crops and new technologies, both of which have been flourishing in Latin America since the liberalization process began. We already mentioned the cut-flower and fern industries, both excellent examples of market opportunities for non-traditional crops. The most important of the new crops has been the counterseasonal fruit and vegetable industries, such as the Chilean winter fruit deal, the Mexican primarily winter vegetable industry and tropical products in much of Latin America, such as mangoes (Brazil, Dominican Republic, Ecuador, Haiti, Mexico, Peru) avocados (Chile, Dominican Republic, and Mexico), pineapple (Dominican Republic, Costa Rica, Honduras and Mexico), orange juice concentrate (Belize, Brazil, Costa Rica, Dominican Republic and Honduras) and many more.

From an entrepreneurial standpoint, agriculture is very much of a "me too" industry. If one farmer buys a new car, his neighbors will emulate him. By financing innovators, we arguably produced a greater developmental impact than just supporting the "me too" imitators.

Like new crops, new technologies can produce many copycats. Mariculture is a good example. Once Chilean investors were persuaded that the Atlantic salmon could be economically grown in sea pens in the waters south of Puerto Montt, money flowed into the industry, which now ships half a billion dollars of salmon a year to international markets, making Chile the world's second largest salmon exporter after Norway. In addition to salmon farming, LAAD also financed oyster and scallops farming in Chile, shrimp farming in Belize, Guatemala, Honduras, Panama, Peru and Venezuela; tilapia farming in Costa Rica and Honduras and a queen conch hatchery in the Turks and Caicos. The seas are clearly being over exploited and fish farming is the only practical alternative to increase production.

The list of new agroindustries financed by LAAD is long and still growing. Aside from the ones already mentioned, they include the berry industry in Chile; soybeans in Bolivia, mangoes in Peru, flowers in Panama, macadamia nuts in Costa Rica, peanuts in Nicaragua, melons and wood products in Honduras, sesame seed and frozen vegetables in Guatemala, pina colada and avocados in the Dominican Republic and plantains in Venezuela. Latin American agriculture is rapidly refocusing its attention.

Agriculture in Latin America has gone through one generation of major, even revolutionary, change by focusing on markets rather than just production. This revolution is far from over and it will continue to bring about structural change in terms of product mix, market focus and the names of the key players. It is quite likely that Latin American agriculture will become increasingly a corporate business just like manufacturing and less of a family affair as it is today. Because of its mission, LAAD will probably stick with the family farmer even as the corporation increases its market share of the total business. The farmer will continue to play an important role, particularly in production of high value crops, but processing and marketing will be gradually taken over by the corporation.

Although LAAD's operations are limited to Latin America, it has been occasionally called upon to provide advice in other parts of the world. AID, the World Bank, the European Union and other development institutions have hired LAAD executives to assist in promoting other agricultural financial institutions in Afghanistan, Central Asia, Philippines, Poland and Sudan. LAAD even seriously considered expanding its concept internationally to Eastern Europe following the collapse of Communism, but the board of directors decided against diluting the company's efforts in Latin America.

9

The Bottom Line:
Profitability and Risk

In most private companies, management seeks to maximize its earnings potential in keeping with its competitive position in the marketplace. In LAAD's case, the prospect of high profits and dividends was not the motivation behind its foundation. Development was the goal, not profits per se.

At the outset, some founders even thought that making money was incompatible with a developmental mission and questioned whether LAAD should even be a profit-making company. Proponents of this view argued that whatever benefits accrued to LAAD from its operations should be returned to the region either by reducing the cost of our money or by providing free technical or similar services. This argument was primarily moral by separating the profit motive from a goal of raising living standards in other countries.

A majority of the founders took the position that profitability was essential to provide the equity base needed for long term growth and to meet our third party obligations. Philosophically, they wanted to strengthen the concept of an open market, free enterprise, and profit-oriented economic system. Free markets allocate resources through the twin mechanisms of price and profits, and for them it was important that LAAD be both a profit-making company as well as a profitable one. Development remained the mission, but it was to be carried out profitably.

From LAAD's point of view, making a profit is important operationally. It encourages efficient management by providing the funding to improve compensation within the company and to pay incentives for good performance. Profitability offers clear budgetary goals for measuring year-end results. It sends a clear signal to LAAD's lenders that it will generate sufficient cash flow to meet its financial commitments. This helps to keep interest rates on LAAD's borrowings down.

These arguments may sound like platitudes to anyone who has taken an introductory course in business, but it once generated controversy in a company whose mission is defined in developmental terms.

Nevertheless, LAAD does not try to maximize profitability from the services it provides. We noted earlier that the board of directors prohibited us from investing in projects that produce alcohol for human consumption, cigarettes or non-agribusiness activities, even if extremely profitable. The board also kept us from straying far from the basic mission of supporting agriculture. Only the processing, storage, shipping, packaging or marketing of farm products has been authorized. The company was not even allowed to finance agricultural chemicals, fertilizers or other agricultural inputs, other than on an exceptional basis. We could have grown faster and more profitably had LAAD been given more freedom to diversify into other economic sectors. Rather than maximize profits, we set out to earn a competitive rate of return, one consistent with prevailing financial conditions and with maintaining a conservative growth in the portfolio.

We are currently seeking to earn an annual return on average net worth of at least 13 percent. This rate of return would hardly cause Wall Street heads to turn given the high risk we are assuming, but at that level of profitability, we approximately match the average return of United States commercial banks of similar size.

In managing our return on equity, we set out from the beginning to establish a trend. Long-term performance was and remains management's financial icon. The average return on net worth for the twenty-six-year period 1973-98 was 9.9 percent. The highest return of 14 percent was achieved in 1984 at the height of the foreign debt crisis. The worst year was 1972, when the company set up loan loss reserves to cover its exposure to two Mexican steel companies, the only such loss in the company's history.

Ironically, our highest returns on net worth were achieved during a period of financial turmoil in Latin America. We took a portion of our cash flow to purchase long-term bonds issued by international development agencies and yielding in excess of 16 percent in U.S. dollars. As interest rates fell in the succeeding years, the market value of these bonds soared and we were able to sell them earning a substantial capital gain. This allowed us to increase loan loss reserves to cover a weakened portfolio and simultaneously show an above-average return on our net worth.

Although LAAD never defaulted on any of its financial obligations, the Latin American debt crisis of the eighties taught us a lesson. From then on, we always maintained a portfolio of high quality internationally marketable bonds equal to 8-10 percent of the portfolio to act as a cushion in case of a recurrence of sovereign defaults in the region.

The payment of dividends was not a motivating factor for the founding shareholders. It was management and not the board of directors that first proposed the payment of a nominal dividend in 1980, ten years after LAAD started operations. That dividend came to $32,000, or 1 percent on invested capital, and it took four years before it was increased. These payments were intended to establish the principle that LAAD would compensate its shareholders for having risked their capital for a long period of time. The dividends made no difference whatsoever to the financial results of our large corporate investors. It was the principal that mattered, not the amount.

Today, LAAD is paying a dividend equal to 30 percent of the par value of its shares and 2.5 percent of its average net worth. The board has set a policy guideline of distributing 25 percent of the previous year's earnings, provided they can be sustained over the long term. Cumulatively, LAAD has paid out dividends of $6.7 million on its common shares, an amount almost three times the company's initial paid-in capital.

One indirect benefit of this dividend policy has been to provide a measurement of share value to a company that is closely held and not traded on any exchange. The payment of a cash dividend creates one benchmark for measuring value. It is clearly much easier for a corporate treasurer to accept a non-core business investment, like LAAD, when he can show that he is receiving a 30 percent annual cash return on his original investment. It is not that the treasurer is against LAAD's mission, but his threshold for holding on to the stock grows concomitantly with pressure for greater shareholder value.

Generating a reasonable return on equity and a growing dividend flow have helped reinforce the viability of the original concept and kept a new generation of managers and directors enthused about LAAD's developmental mission.

Management always recognized that LAAD's business was intrinsically risky. Latin America's record of meeting its international obligations has been historically poor. Agriculture is one of the highest risk economic activities. Our mission required us to absorb both the political as well as the commercial risks fully in our agribusiness portfolio.

This concern with high risk surfaced in many areas. Our directors were particularly concerned with meeting our debt service obligations with AID, which had made six unsecured loans to LAAD totaling nearly $50 million. This was all money coming from the U.S. taxpayer and it would have been extremely embarrassing to our shareholders if we did not make our payments to AID on time. Both management and the directors concurred that LAAD's financial operations should be handled conservatively, even as it made risky loans for agribusiness development.

Financial conservatism was pursued on several fronts. LAAD always kept a low overall debt/equity ratio of no more than 3:1 and a current ratio of 2:1 or higher. These are extremely low ratios for a financial institution, particularly commercial banks which often have 15:1 debt/equity ratios. We matched the tenor of our loans with medium and long term borrowings, even though short-term borrowings are easier and cheaper to obtain. We maintained a close relationship between floating rate loans and floating rate borrowings to avoid being caught in an interest rate squeeze. We hold marketable securities equal to 8-10 percent of the agribusiness portfolio in case of dire emergency. These and other policies have enabled LAAD to meet all of its financial obligations, which were always paid punctually and never rescheduled.

LAAD sets aside loan loss reserves each year to cover potential losses in the portfolio. To date, the company has cumulatively set aside nearly $20 million in reserves, which represent 32 percent of operating profits during that period. Of these, $12 million in loans and investments were written off and $8 million remain as reserves. At the present time, these reserves represent about 7.5 percent of the agribusiness portfolio and 2.5 times the non-performing loan portfolio.

LAAD faces many specific risks, including exchange risk, inconvertibility, expropriation, weather, earthquakes, terrorism, politics, the legal system, the market, and, most importantly, the client himself. Each of these risks has to be considered when making a new loan.

Exchange risk. When the first major wave of devaluations hit countries we operated in, we found ourselves exposed to those projects which sold their production in local currency and were unable to raise their prices as fast as the rate of devaluation. Since their debts with LAAD were denominated in U.S. dollars, they suffered losses, sometimes severe. Over time, they could raise their prices to compensate for the loss in purchasing power, but this process could take years. In many cases, we had to reschedule the debts to give the client more time. In most cases, we eventually recovered the full amount of these loans, but we learned that it is not appropriate to make hard currency loans in inflationary economies to companies which do not sell in hard currency. Consequently, we shifted over to lending exclusively to companies which either generate hard currency, or their sales prices are quoted in dollars.

As inflation becomes less of a problem, we have made a growing number of exceptions, but only after a careful assessment of the risk involved. Hopefully, today's more benign inflationary environment will one day allow LAAD to finance any project based on its merits, and not on its ability to generate hard currency.

Inconvertibility risk. In the early eighties, LAAD suffered a temporary slowdown in its cash inflow when most Latin American countries declared themselves in default and their central banks suspended or at least delayed payments abroad. This risk affected our entire portfolio, including those projects which were generating sufficient foreign exchange to cover their obligations. There is little LAAD can do to avoid this risk other than to remain a good corporate citizen. The company will always be vulnerable to arbitrary decisions by host governments. This risk will remain one of the costs of doing business in Latin America.

Expropriation risk. This risk is usually borne by equity investors, but lenders can also get caught in the middle, as was the case in Nicaragua, when the Sandinista government expropriated all of the businesses that had been financed by LAAD. The company will always remain exposed to the risk of expropriation as it is to inconvertibility. In today's world, these two risks appear rather remote, but politicians are well known to shift with the prevailing winds of public opinion and who knows what the long term will bring.

Weather risk. Adverse weather patterns can and do influence the prices for agricultural commodities. We secretly hope that the pain will be borne by someone else's client, but statistical averages show no favorites. Weather patterns everywhere in the world influence the prices received by our clients. When our clients are affected negatively, the consequences can cause illiquidity if only one year's crop is damaged, but insolvency can result if the damage is longer lasting. In our area of the world, the most damaging weather phenomenon has been hurricanes, which typically affect the Caribbean and the Gulf coasts of Central America. A hurricane will blow down a banana plantation, but production will normally resume in six months or so. A hurricane can also destroy a citrus plantation, which takes much longer to recover. Hurricane Georges in 1998 caused extensive damage to LAAD-financed banana plantations and avocado trees in the Dominican Republic. A few weeks later, Hurricane Mitch doused Honduras and Belize with heavy rains and high winds, causing extensive damage to a LAAD-financed seafood company on the Honduran island of Guanaja and to LAAD's banana, citrus and shrimp farming clients in Belize and Honduras. LAAD responded by rescheduling maturities when needed and providing additional funds to pay for reconstruction. In no case, did insolvency result from either of these storms.

El Nino also causes extensive damage to agriculture up and down the Pacific Coast and sometimes even along the Atlantic side of the Andes. Agriculture usually assumes a predictable weather pattern. Some crops, like tomatoes and melons, prefer dry weather. Others like corn and bananas prefer more rain. When normal rainfall patterns are reversed by El Nino, the short-term damage to annual crops can be substantial. Long-term damage to tree crops is rare, however.

LAAD has typically tried to take an understanding position when one of its clients suffers server weather-induced damage. Sometimes, the borrower will be able to continue servicing his debt with earnings from another business or from past savings. When his only source of income is his farm, LAAD would normally reschedule his loan to fit a tighter projected cash flow and consider additional financing to replant or to rebuild.

Historically, weather-induced risk has been controllable.

Earthquakes. An earthquake damages structures such as processing plants, cold storage facilities and supermarkets. Damage can be severe. The normal protection against this risk is an insurance policy to protect the integrity of physical assets, especially those pledged to guarantee the loan.

Since all of LAAD's mortgage agreements routinely require adequate insurance, this risk has never caused us any losses.

Terrorism. This is one of the most insidious risks. To date terrorism has never caused any physical damage to any of our clients as happens with oil pipelines in Colombia. Terrorism strikes at the business owner, his senior management, and their families. Murder and kidnapping lead the list of risks under this heading. We have had only one case of a client being killed by terrorists and that incident led to a partial write-off of the loan. Kidnapping has hit several of our clients. Payments made to the kidnappers to secure the release of loved ones have reduced our borrowers' net worth and cash flow. We have had to reschedule some of these loans. The danger of murder and kidnapping affects the cost of doing business by requiring expensive security measures, often forcing clients to send their families abroad at a high cost and reducing the attractiveness of investing in rural areas. Terrorism does not affect all of Latin America, but it still remains significant in a number of the countries where we operate.

Political. The political process affects the rules of the game in every country in the world and represents a major uncertainty. However, LAAD looks on this as another market risk. The company rarely stop doing business in a country, because LAAD disagrees with the politics of the ruling party, the extent of government corruption, or even dictatorial rule. LAAD knows enough about the region that it can live within whatever parameters are laid out by the political system. We do not pay bribes to government officials and we do not provide funding for active politicians. We do review the political risk in all the countries where we operate twice a year. Although, we will not normally cease doing business in a country solely for concern about political stability, we may delay or even reduce a specific country limit in the event of extreme political instability.

The legal system. Before we start operating in a country for the first time, we do our own diagnosis of the local legal system, how it works, whether it is corrupt, whether laws can be enforced and how expensive it is to litigate. There is little correlation between the degree of development and the efficiency of the legal system. Probably the most efficient legal system in Latin America is Belize; uncomplicated and to the point. One of the most inefficient is Costa Rica, where even an incompetent lawyer can delay legal proceedings for years and take a case routinely to the Supreme Court on a technicality. Relative to the United States, however, the Latin American legal system is a paradigm of efficiency. LAAD was once sued in federal court in the United States and it took ten years of legal wrangling, one appeal and four different Federal judges before the case was finally thrown out on summary judgment.

LAAD never hired an in-house legal counsel and has relied exclusively on local lawyers. This has proven to be both cost and legally effective, as the company has not lost a single lawsuit. The risk of the Latin American legal system has been more in the cost of delays. A loan that may be adequately collateralized at the time of loan signing, may no longer be so at the end of a long court battle. Not only does the loan outstanding increase with unpaid interest charges, but many types of collateral deteriorate over time, whether it be tree crops or physical facilities.

Market risk. These are the normal commercial risks faced by any commercial enterprise. In the case of export agriculture, the primary market risk is price, which can rarely be influenced by the producer. The prices for agricultural products typically fluctuate more violently than any other economic activity, primarily because weather influences output independently of demand, and price is the only regulator to balance off supply and demand. International commodity prices can easily fluctuate by 25 percent up or down in a single year. LAAD protects itself against the risk of low prices by making certain that its clients are cost efficient in international terms and do not rely on government subsidies to survive. We also do standard sensitivity analyses in our loan proposals to measure the borrower's ability to withstand lower prices.

Our clients. Although the above list of business risks may seem daunting to the casual observer, LAAD's portfolio losses from all of them combined do not equal the risk posed by our clients, and more specifically the owner(s). A competent owner can turn a mediocre project into a success and an incompetent one can drive the best project into bankruptcy. The human factor in our business is at the core of our success or failure. Projects do not repay loans, their owners do.

We have reviewed the reasons why loans went bad and, with the exception of the Sandinista expropriations, the vast majority was the result of bad management, which in the case of small and medium sized companies means the owner.

The key to any business is knowing your client, and this is particularly true in the lending business. LAAD makes mistakes by choosing the wrong borrower. Even when we are fully collateralized, bad borrowers can hire good lawyers and take advantage of legal technicalities to delay a final judgement at considerable cost to both sides.

Often we only have a matter of hours to decide whether a potential client is worth backing. There is certainly an advantage to looking him straight in the eye and asking yourself whether this is the kind of person to entrust your money with. It helps to know his family and his family history. Most rural communities are socially tightly knit. We talk to our older clients about their opinion of potential new ones.

Another technique consists of asking detailed questions about the business. The purpose is to focus on how the question is answered rather than the specifics of the answer This tells you whether the client really knows his business. A lack of knowledge is often an indication of incompetence especially in highly competitive markets. Anyone can hire a consultant to prepare a feasibility study, which is easy to convert into a loan proposal. The issue is to determine how much the owner himself really knows about what he is proposing to do with our money.

Who were LAAD's biggest risk clients? The bulk of our financing has been directed to small and medium private enterprises, typically family owned and managed. Most of these are nationals of the country where we operate. Some of our clients are foreign investors. In some cases, particularly in our early years, we channeled funds through other financial institutions such as government development banks and local commercial banks. During periods of foreign exchange crises, we sometimes found ourselves with having central banks as involuntary clients.

We have looked back to rate the different types of clients we had in terms of risk and particularly where we had to write off bad loans and investments. This analysis resulted in the following ordering of our clients, starting off with the highest risk. We might add that the level of risk is closely correlated with the quality of management; that is, the higher the risk the poorer the management.

Governments. Clearly our highest risk profile is the central government, in this case the Sandinista government in Nicaragua. That government expropriated every project financed by LAAD in the country, mismanaged all of them and defaulted on its renegotiated debt causing us to write off the entire amount of our exposure. This was a classic example of how the political administration of economic assets leads to incompetence.

Central banks. During most of our thirty years in business, central banks imposed exchange controls as a way of managing the countries' available foreign exchange. These exchange controls were typically poorly managed, leading to extensive losses in the central banks themselves and their creditors alike.

Government development banks. We occasionally channeled funding through local development banks, and in most cases, they also defaulted because of poor management, such as lending money to unqualified borrowers for political reasons.

Commercial banks (both public and private). We occasionally channeled money through local commercial banks. Although better managed than the government development banks, the failure level due to poor management was also relatively high and we suffered some losses.

Foreign investors. We found that foreign investors often led the way in innovating new ideas. Since we specialized in nontraditional agricultural exports, we frequently lent money to companies set up by foreign investors, who usually had good market contacts as well as specialized knowledge. While attractive on paper, we found that a good knowledge of local growing conditions and labor relations is often more important than knowledge of markets and technology. Put differently, it is easier to buy the market and technology than to buy local growing and management expertise. The percentage of failure by foreign investors exceeded the rate of failure by local entrepreneurs by a factor of several times. The most successful foreign investors were those who settle down in the country where they do business.

Local businessmen/farmers. This category accounted for the bulk of our investing activities and is the one with the lowest risk. Virtually all of them are family enterprises. In size, they ranged from small farms to medium-sized agroindustrial businesses. Typically, the client's sole source of income came from the project we were financing, a reality which encouraged him to stay focused. Sometimes the client was well educated and trained in his specialty, and sometimes, he learned his business from childhood. Often it was a combination of both. Accounting has not always been his strength. He is rarely audited and never writes an annual report with standard SEC disclosures. Character, determination and hard work are the key traits from our point of view. The individual farmer, rancher, aquaculturalist and industrialist form the core of LAAD's portfolio and are the main reason why our write-offs have been so low in relation to the risk we assume.

Managing these risks has been the key to LAAD's financial performance over the long run. The company is now in a strong position to grow, since it has successfully overcome a full gamut of risks associated with political and financial instability, damaging weather patterns and volatile commodity prices.

10

Development, Politics, and the Human Factor

The international business environment in Latin America has changed dramatically since LAAD was formed back in 1970. These changes have affected agriculture most profoundly. Indeed, it would be fair to say that an economic revolution has taken place, a revolution that continues to this day.

The two most significant changes were the decline in the role of the state in Latin America and a steady decline in protectionism in the industrialized world. The state has lost its paternalistic control over agricultural production and the farmer has again regained his economic independence. Internationally, tariffs on agricultural products are declining and non-tariff barriers to trade are being weakened.

One of the last bastions of mercantilism, the European Union's policy on banana imports, has been rejected by the World Trade Organization and will have to be modified. Many other barriers to agricultural trade remain, but the handwriting is on the wall.

We have seen in the preceding pages countless examples of private entrepreneurship at work throughout Latin America. Agriculture is clearly benefiting from the decline in government control and free trade. LAAD was a minor player in this global play, but we channeled most of our available funds to back projects that would have otherwise never have been proposed without these two major changes in the business environment.

Agriculture is no longer the political wasteland of anachronistic ideologies. Young Latin American entrepreneurs are seeking to make their livelihood by growing crops that can be sold into a global market place. Agriculture offers a significant advantage to a new generation of agribusinessmen—its economies of scale are far less significant than in traditional manufacturing. An investment of a few hundred thousand dollars can create a profitable business sufficient to support a family. Although the financial cost may be low, the knowledge component of agribusiness has multiplied with the opening up of new markets. The new agribusiness entrepreneur has to bring together an international selling capability with an efficient production base and an understanding of local human and physical realities. This is a difficult task, but the number of success stories grows by the day.

As we survey today's almost limitless opportunities, it is easy for us to forget what the world was like barely a generation and a half ago. The grand debate over development strategy was very much in its heyday. It dominated the political agenda of politicians in both authoritarian and democratic nations alike. Looking back with the benefit of hindsight, the debate itself was often worse than the solutions proposed.

A farmer is like an investor on the stock market. His worst enemy is uncertainty. The political debates then were over fundamental issues like property rights, state intervention in the economy and which superpower to be allied with. Governments routinely fixed prices and rigged markets. Investing in any activity was risky and agriculture was the riskiest of all. Latin American politicians were debating not just whether to raise or lower support prices, but whether to expropriate land, nationalize food processing industries, or create government purchasing monopolies. Inflation and devaluations left the farmer wondering what the real value of his harvest would be at the end of the growing season.

Because of this debate, the rational farmer would often opt not to invest in his land, but to buy dollars and invest them in a Miami condominium. He would hire as few workers as possible and produce annual crops with the least risk. Low risk crops would be those destined for the local market or those where international agreements provided some degree of safety at the time.

Politicians would openly criticize the farmers' priorities, but their actions were a perfectly logical response to the politicians' own shifting development strategies. Agricultural production stagnated for decades in Latin America, waiting for this sterile debate to end.

The passing on of the ideological politician in Latin America has opened up a revolutionary new agricultural frontier—the market place. Markets are themselves dynamic and a premium is placed on producers able to serve it efficiently and competitively. The modern-day farmer is an active player in this market. He is at the same time the strength and weakness of the world food chain. He is the strength in that he works the hardest. He is the weakest in that he probably knows the least.

One of today's great challenges is how to integrate the production capacity of even remote communities in Latin America with the global marketplace. This will have to happen if the benefits of the new world order are to reach the rural poor and if the economic revolution is to bring with it a social revolution. Income gaps between the rich and poor, particularly in rural Latin America, remain the Achilles heel of the new world order.

We have repeatedly emphasized the importance that LAAD gives to the reputation and ability of its clients. They "make it happen." We recognize the importance of basic infrastructure in encouraging growth, but that same infrastructure without qualified people able to use it efficiently is a poor investment.

The Ferghana Valley in Uzbekistan has a climate and basic infrastructure comparable to the central valleys of California and Chile. It has roads, railroads, electricity, an extensive irrigation system, a literate work force, and large processing plants. Fruit orchards and irrigated farm land stretch out as far as the eye can see. Unfortunately, the farmers plant the wrong varieties; they have little sense of quality control; productivity is low, and industrial processing follows Soviet tenets of maximizing production with little consideration of markets. Worst of all, the farmers do not understand their problem although they do know that they earn very little money for their work.

Uzbekistan's business leaders learned how to work in a system which issued production decrees from the ministries in Moscow. Now, the market place takes those decisions, and the managers are disoriented. Production is declining, despite all of the heavy investments in infrastructure. What is needed is an equally heavy investment in education, particularly business management.

In Latin America, the rules of the game are still being rewritten. We would argue that the debate on agricultural development should wear a human face. By this we mean that agriculture, more than any other business, depends on an ability to adapt to local micro realities, both climatic and human, and convert these realities into market opportunities. Agriculture and fishing are very locale specific, more like the real estate business. Success depends on understanding and harnessing this local reality to enter the global marketplace.

More than anything else, Latin American agriculture today needs more investment in human capital, starting with primary education for the illiterate children of peasant farmers. There is no economic policy that can take a peasant farmer out of poverty. The market place does not need him. He does not feed the growing urban population and he has no money to buy anything. He is a living anachronism in today's changing world and a sure source of instability into the next century. The options are simple; either make him productive on his land or educate his children and give them the ability to make a living in some other economic activity elsewhere.

This concern with education has to continue all the way to the university level. Agricultural colleges in Latin America have traditionally focused on production technology in order to prepare qualified agronomists. While there is a continuing need for that knowledge, today's agribusiness requires just as much knowledge about accounting, financial analysis, investment alternatives, personnel management, marketing and cutting edge technology as any other field of business. With the demise of government's tutelage toward agriculture and its protection of inefficient farms, agriculture today offers as many attractive career opportunities as any other industry.

Agriculture is integrated into the financial markets through the various commodity exchanges, such as the Chicago Board of Trade, which are open to players from any country in the world. A wheat producer in Argentina, a shrimp farmer in Ecuador and a coffee farmer in Guatemala can all protect their future sales price months before harvest through the futures market. Latin America's farmers need to know how to use these exchanges.

Technology is finally beginning to arrive at the farm gate. No till farming saves as much fuel and topsoil in Brazil as it does in Kansas. Precision farming and chemically tolerant crop varieties save as much agricultural chemicals in the Department of Santa Cruz, Bolivia as in Missouri.

Health safety concerns such as chemical residues mean that standards enforced in consuming nations will be applied to all producing areas on a global basis. This even holds true when different countries enforce different levels of consumer safety. Producers wanting to sell into multiple markets have to grow crops meeting different sets of standards.

Even farm worker safety standards are reaching beyond national boarders with pressure mounting for consuming nations to impose minimum safety standards overseas to nations supplying them with product. Supermarkets in England routinely visit their Latin American suppliers to inspect worker hygiene, living conditions and chemical spraying schedules as part of their overall quality control on behalf of their customers.

Eating habits and consumer tastes differ among countries, age groups and income groups, all of which must be catered to in order to make money in agriculture. Americans like Thompson seedless green grapes, Saudi Arabians like red grapes with the seeds in them. Moscow, Milan, and Minneapolis all buy roses, but not the same varieties. The Japanese buy frozen salmon shipped by sea, Americans prefer fresh salmon shipped by air. The French buy their scallops with the muscle still attached, but they object if foreign producers call them Coquille Saint Jacques. Americans prefer the muscle removed and are delighted to call them Coquille Saint Jacques if that will help fetch a higher price on a menu written in French.

Competition is now global. A successful raspberry grower in Chile has to know what the Costa Rican, Guatemalan, and Mexican growers plan to do in the U.S. market. He has to keep a sharp eye on American growers, who are experimenting with varieties and farm practices allowing them to extend their growing season. In the European market, he has to consider New Zealand, South Africa, and Zimbabwe, all of which sell to Europe in the counter-season. In the frozen raspberry market, he has to pay attention again to Yugoslavia, which used to dominate the frozen berry market in Europe before the recent fighting.

The peasant farmer has no hope of playing a role in this world by himself. Either he finds someone to help him grow higher value crops and sell them to the market place, or he would be better off selling his land and going into another business.

These are some of the basic realities that face farmers, large and small, in the emerging markets and we do not see any retreat back to the old ideologies. Too many people are benefiting, both as consumers and producers. Too many farms are already integrated into the global system to return to autarchy or national self sufficiency.

If we can make one appeal for help from the international development community it is to refocus its attention in solving rural and agricultural problems from government extension services, community development, self help programs, food relief and crop subsidies in favor of education at all levels on a massive scale. The rural poor must learn to read, write, and acquire minimum skills. Above all, they need to think differently. They need to be taught how they can improve their living standards in agriculture.

Agricultural colleges should shift their curricula to teach general business and entrepreneurial skills to enable their graduates to compete internationally. The modern farmer needs to be as computer literate as any other professional; he has to speak one of the world's international languages if he is to understand foreign markets; and above all he has to provide the leadership within his community necessary to organize production around the demands of the market place. The successful farmer will have to be an entrepreneurial one.

LAAD would be honored to finance them.

Appendix A

LAAD's Directors by Shareholder

Adela Investment Company, Lima, Peru   (1970 - 1990)
Alejandro Orfila	(1970 - 1974)
Rafael Morales	(1974 - 1982)
Luis Valenzuela	(1982 - 1984)
F.I. Davies	(1984 - 1990)

Bank of America N.T. & S.A., San Francisco, CA.   (1970 - present)
William H. Bolin	(1970 - 1980)	
Ulrich Merten	(1980 - 1985)	
Robert A. Capwell	(1990 - 1992)	
Roberto Anguizola	(1992 -)	Chairman 1995-96

Borden, Inc., New York, NY   (1970 - present)
John J.O. Connor	(1970 - 1976)
Edward Piernick	(1976 - 1983)
Harry G. Lambroussis	(1983 - 1985)
Joseph M. Saggese	(1985 -)

Cargill, Inc., Minneapolis, MN.   (1970 - present)
H. Robert Diercks	(1970 - 1971)	
John Cole	(1971 - 1976)	Chairman 1973-74
Ricardo Robles	(1976 -)	Chairman 1979-80

Caterpillar Tractor Company, Peoria, IL. (1970 - 1990)

Lee L. Morgan	(1970 - 1973)	
John Montag	(1973 - 1977)	Chairman 1975-76
Mack Verhyden	(1977 - 1984)	
Robert A. Korsgard	(1984 - 1985)	
Earl W. Doubet	(1985 - 1988)	
Michael D. Meadows	(1988 - 1989)	
Ben E. Darrow	(1989 - 1990)	

Centrale Rabobank Curacao N.V.   (1978 - present)

G. N. Brands	(1978 - 1981)	
Gerard J.M. Vlak	(1981 - 1988)	
Hugo Steensma	(1988 - 1992)	
Cor F. Broekhuyse	(1992 - 1994)	
Dennis J. Ziengs	(1994 - 1997)	Chairman 1997
Robert Benoit	(1997 -)	

CPC International, Inc., Englewood Cliffs, NJ. 1_/   (1970 - present)

Ernest W. Hornig	(1970 - 1981)	
Angelo S. Abdela	(1981 - 1997)	Chairman 1987-88
Rainer H. Mimberg	(1997 -)	

Deere & Company, Molina, IL.   (1970 - present)

Robert A. Hanson	(1970 - 1978)
David H. Stowe	(1978 - 1982)

Dow Chemical Company   (1970 - 1974)

German Alvarez-Fuentes	(1970 - 1974)

Gerber Products Company, Fremont, MI. 2_/
(1970 - present)

Frank A. Meyer	(1970 - 1984)	Chairman 1977-78
Donald L. Hanson	(1984 - 1990)	Chairman 1989
Frank Kelly	(1990 - 1995)	Chairman 1993-94
Jack Butterick	(1995 -)	

Girard International Bank, New York, NY. (1975 - 1990)
    Charles M Vollmer   (1975 - 1987)
                                   Chairman 1983-84
    Gerardo P. van Tienhoven   (1987 - 1990)

Monsanto Company, St. Louis, MO.   (1970 - present)
    William J. McCarville   (1970 - 1971)
    Nicholas L. Reding   (1971 - 1972)
    S. Peter Karlow   (1972 - 1973)
    Nicholas L. Reding   (1973 - 1976)
    John B. Lewis   (1976 - 1984)
    Milton P. Wilkins   (1984 - 1986)
    Fred G. Sutton   (1986 - 1998)
                                   Chairman 1991-92
    Carlos A. Buzio   (1998 -   )

Ralston Purina Company, St. Louis, MO. (1970 - present)
    Paul F. Cornelsen   (1970 - 1976)
                                   Chairman 1972-73
    Travis H. Mullenix   (1976 - 1983)
                                   Chairman 1981-82
    Louis A.Van Houten   (1983 - 1985)
    Antonio Vilar   (1985 - 1993)
    Gonzalo J. Dal Borgo   (1993 -   )
                                   Chairman 1998-99

Standard Fruit & Steamship Company, San Francisco, CA. 3_/
(1970 - present)
    Donald J. Kirchhoff   (1970 - 1982)
                                   Chairman 1970-72
    Michael Rotolo   (1982 - 1986)
    David D. DeLorenzo   (1986 - 1992)
    Jerry Vriesenga   (1992 - 1996)
    Juergen Schumacher   (1996 -   )

The Chase Manhatten Bank, New York, NY.
(1972 - present)

Jonathan S. Tobey	(1972 - 1976)
Warren R. Leonard	(1976 - 1997)
	Chairman 1985-86
Brian D. O'Neill	(1998 -)

The First National Bank of Miami, Miami, FL.
(1973 - 1998)

Stanfield S. Taylor	(1973 - 1977)
Sheila Trifari	(1977 - 1982)
Alden S. Blackstone	(1982 - 1983)
Thomas B. Walker	(1983 - 1984)
Oakley W. Cheney Jr.	(1984 - 1985)
William Dewey, III	(1985 - 1988)
Clovis Estorilio	(1988 - 1990)
William A. Brandt, Jr.	(1994 - 1998)

The Goodyear Tire and Rubber Company, Akron, OH.
(1974 - present)

Clarence J. Alameda	(1974 - 1981)
J. F. Corcoran	(1981 - 1985)
Alan L. Ockene	(1985 - 1990)
	Chairman 1990
Richard Johnson	(1990 - 1993)
Christopher Clark	(1993 - 1996)
Kenneth Earhart	(1996 -)

1_/	Now Bestfoods
2_/	Now Novartis Consumer Health
3_/	Now Dole Food Company, Inc.

Appendix B

Selected Financial Indicators 1972-98

	EPS	ROE	ROA	Current Ratio Profit	Op. Exp./ Gross	Reserve/ Portfolio	Earnings ($000,000)	Portfolio
1972	(404)	N.A.	N.A.	-	106	3.0	(.2)	1.5
1973	93	1.9	0.9	-	74	3.9	-	5.0
1974	280	5.3	2.2	-	53	3.1	.2	7.3
1975	303	5.0	1.9	-	64	3.0	.2	9.5
1976	346	5.7	0.8	-	57	2.7	.3	14.1
1977	472	6.9	2.3	5.3:1	51	2.9	.4	18.1
1978	667	8.0	2.7	5.6:1	43	2.7	.5	20.1
1979	931	10.0	2.8	2.1:1	39	3.5	.7	30.0
1980	904	9.4	2.3	2.4:1	40	4.8	.7	32.4
1981	1,453	12.8	3.1	2.2:1	34	6.7	1.1	36.9
1982	1,575	12.3	2.9	2.1:1	33	9.2	1.1	41.9
1983	1,802	12.7	3.0	2.1:1	33	12.0	1.3	44.0
1984	2,231	14.0	3.5	2.3:1	36	12.4	1.6	46.7
1985	2,290	13.0	3.5	2.0:1	41	12.7	1.7	47.5
1986	2,415	12.8	3.7	2.5:1	38	13.6	1.7	43.2
1987	2,263	11.0	3.4	2.5:1	42	12.5	1.5	45.5
1988	2,540	11.1	3.4	2.4:1	43	9.5	1.6	50.1
1989	2,378	9.7	2.9	2.5:1	46	8.6	1.5	42.4
1990	2,709	9.5	2.9	2.6:1	43	8.9	1.6	42.3
1991	2,602	7.8	2.4	2.0:1	48	8.8	1.4	46.3
1992	3,381	9.4	2.8	2.6:1	46	8.4	1.8	49.4
1993	3,937	10.2	3.0	2.0:1	44	7.6	2.0	59.0
1994	4,789	11.4	3.1	2.5:1	43	6.6	2.5	71.1
1995	4,770	10.4	2.8	2.0:1	47	6.6	2.5	80.2
1996	6,322	12.6	3.5	2.2:1	41	6.9	3.3	87.6
1997	7,018	12.7	3.7	2.0:1	41	7.1	3.7	90.0
1998	7,946	13.0	3.8	2.3:1	40	7.4	4.0	96.4

Appendix C

Agribusiness Portfolio by Country
(In order of present holdings)

October 31, 1998
(US$'OOO)

Country	#of Projects	Present Holdings	Percentage of Holdings
Ecuador	25	14,168	14.4
Dominican Republic	56	13,666	13.9
Bolivia	53	13,299	13.4
Guatemala	132	12,089	12.3
Honduras	76	9,246	9.4
Costa Rica	78	8,120	8.2
Nicaragua	33	7,933	8.0
Belize	33	5,235	5.3
Peru	20	3,462	3.5
Venezuela	6	3,200	3.2
Panama	69	3,054	3.1
Colombia	11	2,244	2.3
El Salvador	26	1,370	1.4
Chile	42	549	0.6
St. Vincent	4	494	0.5
Paraguay	1	411	0.4
Haiti	13	1	-
Other	15	0	-
TOTAL	693	314,319 98,541	100.0

Appendix D

Agribusiness Portfolio by Industry
(In order of present holdings)

October 31, 1998
(US$'000)

Industry	# of Projects	Present Holdings	Percentage of Holdings
Fruits and Vegetables	193	36,316	36.8
Cut Flowers	72	13,866	14.1
Food Processing	81	11,455	11.6
Grains	64	11,287	11.4
Agriculture	66	8,438	8.6
Cattle	49	4,874	4.9
Fishing	33	3,923	4.0
Wood Products	28	3,422	3.5
Hogs and Poultry	18	1,975	2.0
Miscellaneous	39	1,650	1.7
Farm Equipment	10	668	0.7
Marketing Services	17	500	0.5
Dairy Products	4	167	0.2
Vegetable Oils	13	-	-
Agrotechnology	6	-	-
TOTAL	693	98,541	100.0

Index

Aceros Ecatapec, 50
Aconex, 70
Adela Investment Company, 2-3,
    12-13, 17, 35, 145
Agency for International Devel-
    opment (AID)
    capitalization
        project expansion, 53-57,
            58, 63, 94, 98-99
        project formation, 1, 12,
            18-21, 35
    debt crisis and, 77, 84-85
Agnelli, Gianno, 2
Agro Austral, 85
AGRODEX, 106-7
Agropecuaria, La Providencia,
    94
Alimentos Amolonca, 48-49
Alimentos Centroamericanos
    (ALCOSA), 44-46
Alliance for Progress (U.S.),
    9-13
Alvarez, Oscar, 32-33
American Flower Corporation,
    42-44
Argentina, 11
    foreign exchange earnings,
        110
Asparagus industry (Peru),
    90-91

Banana industry (Ecuador), 93
Banco Exterior de Espana, 96

Bank of America, 3, 6-7, 16, 145
Bank of Boston, 96
Bank of Tokyo, 97-98
Bankruptcy, 112-13
Banks. *See also specific banks*
    commercial banks
        capitalization and, 95-98
        risk assessment, 132-33
    risk assessment
        central banks, 132
        commercial banks, 132-33
        government development
            banks, 132
Barclays Bank (Great Britain),
    95-96
Barros, Fernando, 70
Beef industry
    Belize, 62-63
    Costa Rica, 47-48
    Nicaragua, 48, 87
Belize
    beef industry, 62-63
    citrus industry, 62-63
    foreign exchange earnings,
        110
Berckmans, Bruce, 21
Berry industry (Chile), 105
Best Foods, 7, 146, 148
Board of Directors, 28-30
    appointment of, 15, 28
    duties, 28
    equal participation, 29
    ethics, 28

marketing advice, 29
mission, 30
shareholder directors, 145-48
Bolin, Bill, 6
Bolivia, 13
  debt crisis, 81
  project expansion, 85, 88-90
    capitalization, 88
  soybean industry, 89-90
Borden, Inc., 3, 145
Brazil, 11
  foreign exchange earnings,
    109-10

Campos Hermanos, 50-51
Capitalization
  Agency for International De-
    velopment (AID)
    project expansion, 53-57,
      58, 63, 94, 98-99
    project formation, 1, 12,
      18-21, 35
  International Finance Corpo-
    ration (IFC), 17
  Overseas Private Investment
    Corporation (OPIC), 17
  project expansion, 53-57, 58,
    63-64, 94-99
    Agency for International
      Development (AID),
      53-57, 58, 63, 94,
      98-99
    Barclays Bank (Great Brit-
      ain), 95-96
    CBI General Partners,
      Inc., 94-95
    commercial banks, 95-98

FUNDAPRO (Bolivia),
    88
  Panamanian bonds, 95
  shareholders, 55-56,
    63-64
shareholders
  project expansion, 55-56,
    63-64
  project formation, 3-4,
    6-7, 15-16
  U.S. government, 7-8, 17-21
Cardamom industry (Guatemala),
    86
Cargill, Inc., 3, 24-25, 145
Caribbean, 56-57, 59-63
Caribex Dominicana, 61
Caterpillar Tractor Company, 3,
    146
CBI General Partners, Inc.,
    94-95
Chase Manhattan Bank, 4, 50, 148
Checa, Jorge, 91
Checchi & Company, 53-54
Chile, 9, 11, 13
  berry industry, 105
  debt crisis, 70-72
    recovery from, 76, 78, 81
    reforestation, 71
    winter fruit market, 70-71
  foreign exchange earnings,
    110, 111
  salmon industry, 104-5, 116
Citrus industry (Belize), 62-63
Client selection, 36-39
  client attitude, 38-39
  risk assessment, 37-38,
    130-32

Cold War
  Alliance for Progress (U.S.),
    9-13
  Communism, 12
  Latin America poverty, 10-11,
    13
  private enterprise support,
    1-2, 9-14
Colombia, 57
  foreign exchange earnings,
    110
Colvin, Sergio May, 71
Communism, 12
Costa Rica
  debt crisis, 66
  early projects
    beef industry, 47-48
    floriculture, 42-44
  foreign exchange earnings,
    110
  ornamental plant industry, 86
  project expansion, 85-86
CPC International, Inc., 4, 7, 146
Crop Genetics International,
  78-79
Cuba, 110
Currency exchange, 124-25

Dairy industry (Honduras), 59
Deere & Company, 4, 7, 146
Dole Food Company, 17, 24, 93,
  147, 148
Dominican Republic, 60-61
Dorn, Reid, 71
Dow Chemical Company, 4, 49,
  146
Dresdner Bank Lateinamerika, 96

Earthquakes, 127-28
Economic Commission for Latin
  America (ECLA), 10
Ecuador
  debt crisis, 81
  foreign exchange earnings,
    110
  project expansion, 85
    banana industry, 93
    floriculture, 92-93
Education
  project impact on, 139-40,
    142-43
  of project management, 30,
    32, 33, 34
El Salvador, 13
  debt crisis, 75
  politics of, 66-67
  sesame seed industry, 48
Employment opportunities,
  102-9
  berry industry, 105
  floriculture, 103-4, 106-7
  salmon industry, 104-5, 116
  wage exploitation, 108-9
  weather conditions and,
    108-9
Expropriation, 126
Eyzeguirre, Jorge, 71

Fernandez, Benjamin, 32
Fig industry (Peru), 91
First National Bank of Miami,
  50, 148
Flambert, Frantz, 61-62
Flores de la Montana, 93
Floriculture

Costa Rica, 42-44
ornamental plant industry, 86
Ecuador, 92-93
employment opportunities from, 103-4, 106-7
Haiti, 61-62
Foreign exchange earnings, 102-3, 109-14
Argentina, 110
bankruptcy, 112-13
Belize, 110
Brazil, 109-10
Chile, 110, 111
Colombia, 110
Costa Rica, 110
Cuba, 110
Ecuador, 110
Guatemala, 110
import substitution, 10, 110-11
inflation, 112-13
nontraditional agriculture, 111-12
project impact on, 113-14
Foreign investors, 133
Frente Sandinista de Liberacion Nacional (FSLN), 65-70
Fruit juice production (Dominican Republic), 61
Fruticola Agricola del Sur, 91
FUNDAPRO (Bolivia), 88

Gelfman, Daniel, 106-7
Gerber Products Company, 4, 146
Girard Bank, 4, 50, 147

Globalism
project development and, 117-18
project formation and, 5
project impact on, 138-39, 141-42
Goodyear Tire and Rubber Company, 4, 25, 50, 148
Grape industry (Peru), 91
Guatemala, 17
debt crisis, 75-76
early projects
mushroom production, 46-47
vegetable freezing, 44-46
foreign exchange earnings, 110
politics of, 66-67
project expansion
cardamom industry, 86
sesame seed industry, 86

Haiti, 57, 59-60
floriculture, 61-62
Halom, James, 18
Hanover Brands, 44-46
Harker, Arturo, 93
Health safety, 140-41
Honduras
dairy industry, 59
debt crisis, 66
project expansion, 85
winter melon market, 86

Inconvertibility, 125-26
Industrias Amerrisque, 87
Industrias de Aceite, 90

Industrias Nacionales Agricolas, 87-88
Inflation, 112-13, 125
International Basic Economy Corporation, 13
International Finance Corporation (IFC), 17
International Monetary Fund (IMF), 11

Javits, Jacob, 1

Keller, Ernst, 2
Kennedy, John F., 11, 13
Kimball, Frank, 19
Kirchhoff, Don, 17

Latin America. *See also* Cold War; *specific countries*
agribusiness portfolio
by country, 150
by industry, 151
Communism, 12
land ownership, 10-11
poverty, 10-11, 13
project impact on, 135-43
agrarian reform, 12, 13-14, 135-38
development strategy, 136-38
education, 139-40, 142-43
free trade, 135-36
futures market, 140
global market, 138-39, 141-42
health safety, 140-41
human factor, 139-43
state role, 135-36
technology, 140
social reform, 9, 13, 14
state role, 10, 11, 135-36
Latin America, debt crisis of
Bolivia, 81
Chile, 70-72
debt recovery, 76, 78, 81
reforestation, 71
winter fruit market, 70-71
Costa Rica, 66
Ecuador, 81
El Salvador
debt recovery, 75
politics of, 66-67
Guatemala
debt recovery, 75-76
politics of, 66-67
Honduras, 66
Mexico, 72-73
Nicaragua
debt recovery, 76-77
foreign debt moratorium, 67-68
payment rescheduling, 68-69
politics of, 65-70, 85, 86-87, 132
Peru, 75
politics and
Costa Rica, 66
El Salvador, 66-67
Guatemala, 66-67
Honduras, 66
Nicaragua, 65-70, 85, 86-87, 132
recovery from, 74-85

Agency for International Development (AID), 77, 84-85
Bolivia, 81
bonds, 80, 81
Chile, 76, 78, 81
Crop Genetics International, 78-79
Ecuador, 81
El Salvador, 75
geographic diversification, 80-81
Guatemala, 75-76
Nicaragua, 76-77
Peru, 75
Plant Resources Venture Fund II, 78-79
project investments, 78-80
Leche y Derivados, S. A., 59
Legal system
project expansion and, 58
risk assessment, 129-30
Leyde, 59
Lozano, German Torres, 106-7
Maffrey, August, 16
Mango industry (Peru), 91
Maniceros de Nicaragua, 87-88
Mantica, Humberto, 48
Market advice
by Board of Directors, 29
by shareholders, 24-25
Market price, 130
Market value (shares), 27
Martin, J. Hunter, 33
Mellon Bank, 4
Melo, Don Arturo, 85-86
Mexico, 21

debt crisis, 72-73
Miquel, Edmundo, 70
Monge, Andres Cardenas, 93
Monsanto Company, 4, 147
Mooney, Thomas, 17-18, 21, 34-35
Moore, George, 2
Morales, Rafael, 51
Mushroom production (Guatemala), 46-47

Netzlaff, Arno, 89
Nicaragua
debt crisis
foreign debt moratorium, 67-68
payment rescheduling, 68-69
recovery from, 76-77
early projects
beef industry, 48
vegetable freezing, 48-49
politics of, 65-70, 85, 86-87, 132
project expansion, 85, 86-88
beef industry, 87
peanut industry, 87-88
Novales, Alfonso, 46-47
Novartis Consumer Health, 146, 148

Orth, Fred, 6-7, 16
Overseas Private Investment Corporation (OPIC), 17

Panama
poultry production, 44

project expansion, 85
capitalization, 95
Peanut industry (Nicaragua), 87-88
Peru, 13
    debt crisis, 75
    project expansion, 85, 90-92
        asparagus industry, 90-91
        fig industry, 91
        grape industry, 91
        mango industry, 91
Philips, Frederik, 2
Pinochet, Augusto, 70
Plantain industry (Venezuela), 94
Plant Resources Venture Fund II, 78-79
Politics
    Costa Rica, 66
    El Salvador, 66-67
    Guatemala, 66-67
    Honduras, 66
    Nicaragua, 65-70, 85, 86-87, 132
    risk assessment, 128-29
Poultry production (Panama), 44
Prebisch, Raul, 10
Private Investment Company for Asia (PICA), 2
Profitability
    dividends, 122-23
    financial indicators, 149
    importance of, 119-20
    project formation and, 5, 6, 16
    project management and, 15-16, 25, 27, 120-21
    project mission and, 119-20

return rates, 121-22

Rabat, Jose, 70-71
Rabobank Nederland, 4, 63-64, 96, 146
Ralston Purina Company, 4, 7, 24, 147
Ravelo, Carlos Julio, 33, 34
Risk assessment
    central banks, 132
    client selection, 37-38, 130-32
    commercial banks, 132-33
    currency exchange, 124-25
    debt obligations, 123-24
    earthquakes, 127-28
    expropriation, 126
    foreign investors, 133
    by general management, 30
    government development banks, 132
    governments, 132
    inconvertibility, 125-26
    legal system, 129-30
    local businessmen, 133-34
    market price, 130
    politics, 128-29
    project formation and, 4-5
    terrorism, 128
    weather conditions, 91-92, 126-27
Rodriquez, Miguel Angel, 47-48
Romero, Dionisio, 90

Salmon industry (Chile), 104-5, 116
Servicio Agricola Gurdian, 87-88
Sesame seed industry

El Salvador, 48
Guatemala, 86
Societe Internationale pour le Financement de l'Investisement en Afrique (SIFIDA), 2
Somoza, Anastasio, 65-66, 67
Southeast Banking Corporation, 4
Southland Frozen Foods, 61
Soybean industry (Bolivia), 89-90
Standard Fruit and Steamship Company, 4, 17, 147

Technology
    as development priority, 116
    project impact on, 140
Terrorism, 128
Thomas, Michael, 42-44, 85-86

Uzbekistan, 138-39

Varela, Alvaro, 93
Vegetable freezing
    Guatemala, 44-46
    Nicaragua, 48-49
Venezuela
    project expansion, 85, 93-94
        plantain industry, 94

W. R. Grace & Company, 18
Wallenberg, Marcus, 2
Weather conditions
    employment opportunities and, 108-9
    risk assessment and, 91-92, 126-27
Weill, Roberto, 94
Winter fruit market
    Chile, 70-71
    Honduras, 86
World Bank, 1
World Trade Organization, 5